HOW TO WIN CUSTOMERS AND KEEP THEM FOR LIFE

"Unlike many books on selling, this one stresses that it is possible to 'make the sale' but still lose the customer. LeBoeuf includes 10 'problem' sales situations and suggests how best to handle each. His message—'keep the customer happy'—is a simple one. (Maybe more people will heed it!)"

—*Library Journal*

"LeBoeuf's 10 action-ready strategies are the commandments of managing 'the moment of truth'—those moments of customer contact."

—Jere W. Thompson, President and CEO,
The Southland Corporation

"In *Getting Results!*, which has been hailed as one of the most important business and management books of the decade, LeBoeuf details how managers can get the most from their employees, their peers, even their employers. *How to Win Customers and Keep Them for Life* takes the lessons of *Getting Results!* one step further..."

—*Northwest* magazine

DON'T MISS MICHAEL LeBOEUF'S CLASSIC...*GETTING RESULTS!*

"The search for excellence is over! Michael LeBoeuf has captured it, simplified it, delivered it, so we can live and build it in others."

—Dr. Denis Waitley, author of *The Double Win*

Berkley Books by Michael LeBoeuf

GETTING RESULTS!
HOW TO WIN CUSTOMERS AND KEEP THEM FOR LIFE
IMAGINEERING

HOW TO WIN CUSTOMERS
AND KEEP THEM FOR LIFE

MICHAEL LeBOEUF, Ph.D.

BERKLEY BOOKS, NEW YORK

This Berkley book contains the complete
text of the original hardcover edition.

HOW TO WIN CUSTOMERS AND KEEP THEM FOR LIFE

A Berkley Book / published by arrangement with
G. P. Putnam's Sons

PRINTING HISTORY
G. P. Putnam's Sons edition / January 1988
Berkley trade paperback edition / March 1989

ISBN: 0-425-11468-6

A BERKLEY BOOK ® TM 757,375
Berkley Books are published by The Berkley Publishing Group,
200 Madison Avenue, New York, New York 10016.
The name "BERKLEY" and the "B" logo
are trademarks belonging to Berkley Publishing Corporation.
PRINTED IN THE UNITED STATES OF AMERICA

20 19 18 17 16 15

ACKNOWLEDGMENTS

With special thanks to:

Artie and Richard Pine for their loyalty, friendship, enthusiasm, and support. You guys will make a writer out of me yet.

Adrienne Ingrum for being an outstanding editor and a wonderful person to work with.

My friends and colleagues of The National Speakers Association for giving me a multitude of ideas and stories to help make this a more useful and entertaining book.

The numerous companies and executives who generously shared their ideas and experiences with me.

To Artie Pine

who knows how to win authors and keep them for life.

Contents

Are "Nice Customers" Ruining Your Business?   11
Something to Think About   13
An Essential Introduction   15

PART ONE. THE BASICS

1. The Greatest Business Secret in the World   23
2. Better Than Selling   29
3. The Greatest Customer You'll Ever Win   34
4. The Only Two Things People Ever Buy   38
5. They'll Buy Much More When They Buy You   45
6. The Customer's Perception Is Everything   51
7. To Win New Customers, Ask the Golden Question   59
8. To Keep Customers for Life, Ask the Platinum Questions   65
9. The Five Best Ways to Keep Customers Coming Back   74

PART TWO. MANAGING THE MOMENTS OF TRUTH: TEN ACTION-READY STRATEGIES

Introduction   81

What to Do When the Customer:

10. Appears, Calls, or Inquires   83
11. Is Angry or Defensive   91
12. Has Special Requests   97
13. Can't Make Up His Mind   102

14.	Raises Obstacles or Objections to Buying	107
15.	Gives Buying Signals	116
16.	Buys	122
17.	Refuses to Buy	127
18.	Complains	133
19.	Is Going to Be Disappointed	139
	Summing Up Part Two. To Manage Any Moment of Truth, Ask the Winning Question	143

PART THREE. THE TRIPLE-WIN REWARD SYSTEM

	Introduction	147
20.	What Gets Rewarded Gets Done	148
21.	How to Keep the Spotlight on the Customer	154
22.	The Quality Customer Service Action Plan	165
	Epilogue	178
	Summary of How to Win Customers and Keep Them for Life	179
	Postscript	182
	Index	184

Are "Nice Customers" Ruining Your Business?

I'm a nice customer. You all know me. I'm the one who never complains, no matter what kind of service I get.

I'll go into a restaurant and sit quietly while the waiters and waitresses gossip and never bother to ask if anyone has taken my order. Sometimes a party that came in after I did gets my order, but I don't complain. I just wait.

And when I go to a store to buy something, I don't throw my weight around. I try to be thoughtful of the other person. If a snooty salesperson gets upset because I want to look at several things before making up my mind, I'm just as polite as can be. I don't believe rudeness in return is the answer.

The other day I stopped at a full service gas station and waited for almost five minutes before the attendant took care of me. And when he did, he spilled gas and wiped the windshield with an oily rag. But did I complain about the service? Of course not.

I never kick. I never nag. I never criticize. And I wouldn't dream of making a scene, as I've seen some people do in public places. I think that's uncalled for. No, I'm the nice customer. And I'll tell you who else I am.

I'm the customer who never comes back!

—Author unknown
(but nice)

Something to Think About

1. A typical business hears from only 4 percent of its dissatisfied customers. The other 96 percent just quietly go away and 91 percent will never come back. That represents a serious financial loss for companies whose people don't know how to treat customers, and a tremendous gain to those that do.

2. A survey on "Why customers quit" found the following:

- 3 percent move away
- 5 percent develop other friendships
- 9 percent leave for competitive reasons
- 14 percent are dissatisfied with the product
- *68 percent quit because of an attitude of indifference toward the customer by the owner, manager or some employee.*

3. A typical dissatisfied customer will tell eight to ten people about his problem. One in five will tell twenty. It takes twelve positive service incidents to make up for one negative incident.

4. Seven out of ten complaining customers will do business with you again if you resolve the complaint in their favor. If you resolve it on the spot, 95 percent will do business with you again. On average, a satisfied complainer will tell five people about the problem and how it was satisfactorily resolved.

5. The average business spends six times more to attract new customers than it does to keep old ones. Yet customer loyalty is in most cases worth ten times the price of a single purchase.

6. Businesses having low service quality average only a 1 percent return on sales and lose market share at the rate of 2 percent per year. Businesses with high service quality average a 12 percent return on sales, gain market share at the rate of 6 percent per year and charge significantly higher prices.

An Essential Introduction

Be it furniture, clothes, or health care, many
industries today are marketing nothing more than
commodities—no more, no less. What will make
the difference in the long run is the care and
feeding of customers.

—MICHAEL AND TIMOTHY MESCON

How to Win Customers and Keep Them for Life is much, much more
than just another treatise about how to smile and be nice to customers. It's a handbook for transforming the people of any size organization into a customer-driven, turned-on team.

One of the single greatest keys to long-term business success can
be summed up in three simple words: *quality customer service.* Yet
as customers, you and I are painfully aware that outstanding service
is far too rare. Why is excellent service so rare? Basically, there are
three problems involved.

1. Employees don't know the basics. All too often, employees
having contact with customers are sent out to perform a job without
a clear understanding of what it takes to create and keep customers.
A lot of potential business is lost simply because employees don't
know any better.

**2. The moments of truth—those crucial points of customer contact
that can make or break a business—are not being properly identified
and managed.** Every time a customer comes into contact with a
company, he comes away feeling better or worse about it. And it's
how well employees manage those numerous moments of truth
every day that ultimately determines how successful the business

will be. Resolve a complaining customer's problem on the spot and the odds are nineteen to one that he will do business with you again. Mishandle the complaint and you lose him forever, not to mention the eight to ten people he will tell.

3. The reward system. Quite simply, excellent service is rare because most managers fail to reward workers for giving excellent service. The typical business hires a person to do a job, pays him a flat wage, and gives him little or no incentive to go that extra mile for the customer. And in that type of climate, the typical employee attitude degenerates to one of indifference or even contempt toward the customer: "You gotta problem, Mac? Call customer service. That's what they're paid for. I tell ya, this would be a great place to work if the customers wouldn't keep screwing things up."

Of course, customers rarely get such a rude message in words. Instead, the employee's behavior delivers the message loud and clear. Yet to the customer, that employee *is* the company. And that customer will likely take his dollars elsewhere in the future. The goal of this book is to make sure this won't happen where you work, because if it happens often enough, where you work won't exist anymore.

While the focus of this book is on creating and keeping customers for life, you won't, of course, always win or keep them all for life any more than you will always bowl a perfect score or shoot par every time you play golf. But if you follow the ideas in this book, I guarantee that you'll find yourself winning and keeping more customers than ever. And striving to make every customer and potential customer a lifetime partner is a goal that will do wonders for any company and any employee that chooses to pursue it.

You may be thinking, "That sounds great if you're an owner, executive or some big wheel, but I just work here on a salary and don't plan to be here forever. Why should I learn how to win customers and keep them for life? There's nothing in it for me."

Well, unless you're planning a fast, permanent exit from the work world, I've got news for you. Knowing how to win and keep customers is the single most important business skill that anyone can learn. Master this one skill and there are literally thousands of businesses that can make you rich. Your age, sex, race, religion, or ethnic background won't matter. The business world makes way for the person who brings the dollars in the door. And that's the person who wins and keeps customers. If you someday plan to open your own business, your ultimate success will depend on how many customers you win and keep. No matter what your current lot in life is, taking the time to learn this one skill is the most profitable investment of your time you can make.

The way to winning and keeping customers is to solve the three problems previously mentioned. In the final analysis, problems are disguised opportunities. Hence, this book is divided into three main parts, with each part addressing one of the problems.

In Part One you'll learn the fundamentals of creating and keeping customers. It teaches you such things as:

- The simple but often overlooked reason that customers buy and come back
- A much less stressful approach to creating customers than traditional selling
- The greatest customer you'll ever win
- The only two things people really buy
- How to be the type of person customers like to buy from and how to turn your own unique personality into your greatest asset
- How to make customers recognize and appreciate the fine service you give them
- A simple question that when correctly answered can make anyone rich
- Two more simple questions whose answers will lead the way to repeat business and lifetime customers
- The five best ways to keep customers coming back

Next, you'll learn how to master the moments of truth—those make-or-break points of crucial customer contact. Whenever a customer:

- Appears, calls, or agrees to see you
- Is angry or defensive
- Has special requests
- Can't make up his mind
- Raises obstacles or objections
- Gives buying signals

- Buys
- Refuses to buy
- Complains
- Is going to be disappointed

you'll know how to turn that moment of truth into a positive experience that will make the customer buy and keep coming back. It's all spelled out and waiting for you in Part Two.

Finally, Part Three gives you a step-by-step action plan for creating a customer-driven reward system at work. If you're an owner or manager, or someday hope to be one, this final section is invaluable. It provides an easy-to-follow blueprint that will get everyone in your organization committed to winning, serving, and keeping customers as their top priority. I call this action plan the triple-win reward system, because when it's done correctly there's something in it for everybody. The customers, the employees, and the company all win. And isn't that what good business is all about?

As you can see, this is a short book with short chapters. And it's written that way for several reasons. One is to save you time. Another is so you'll read the whole book. I know that most people who buy business books read only a chapter or two, and I want you to read this one from cover to cover. This information and your time are too valuable to waste.

The chapters are short for two reasons. First, it enables you to read an entire chapter when you have only five or ten minutes to spare and want to use the time productively. And second, short chapters make it easy to use the book later as a reference when you have a particular problem. No, you can't stop and refer to the book when you have an angry customer screaming in your face. But you can refer to it afterward and decide how to prevent or better handle that kind of situation in the future.

You'll get the most from this book if you follow this six-point program:

1. Be an active reader. Read the book slowly with a pencil, pen, or highlighter in your hand. Highlight key passages and make notes to yourself in the margin. If you think something is particularly important, dog-ear the page or write the page number in the front of the book.

2. Make a photocopy of the summary on pages 179–181 and put it somewhere where you will see it frequently every day.

3. After reading the entire book, spend a few minutes each day and page through the book noting the high points you marked. The key to applying knowledge habitually is to get it ingrained in your subconscious. And the way to ingrain it is through spaced repetition.

4. Look at your job and try to identify your most important moments of truth. Then write a brief game plan for managing each one in the future.

5. If you are an owner or manager, meet with your employees, share this information with them, and use it to design your own triple-win reward system. Get each of them a copy of this book. That may sound expensive but it's a whole lot cheaper than losing customers. If just one idea in this book prevents the loss of only one customer or results in the creation of just one lifetime customer, the investment will pay for itself many times over.

6. Take action and follow up. Put these ideas into action and encourage others to do the same. Have everyone, yourself included, keep a log and briefly write down incidents, recording what's actually being done to win and keep customers. Encourage employees to share their incidents, ideas, and problems and give them plenty of positive recognition and praise when they do.

In today's service-oriented economy, excellent service is more than a competitive weapon—it's a survival skill. And those institutions without it run the high risk of going the way of the steam locomotive, the horse and buggy, and the slide rule. Rest assured that if you don't provide it, someone else will. So without further delay, let's get started and learn the greatest business secret in the world. It's the most powerful single guiding principle for winning and keeping customers, and it's the foundation for the rest of this book. Can you afford not to learn it?

Part One
THE BASICS

1

THE GREATEST BUSINESS SECRET IN THE WORLD

Society is always taken by surprise at any new example of common sense.

—RALPH WALDO EMERSON

If I simply told you the Greatest Business Secret, you'd probably just yawn and say, "Everybody knows that." Then you'd forget it. And judging from the quality of service in many businesses today, that's exactly what most of us have done. Yet my years of research and work with organizations have convinced me that the ones that enjoy long-term prosperity do so because they have a consistent-willingness to reexamine and improve on basic factors that others regard as obvious. And perhaps the most obvious and overlooked of all is the value of a satisfied customer.

Stop for a moment and consider just how valuable customers are. They alone make it possible for you to earn your livelihood in the way that you do. Treat them well and satisfied customers will be your best source of advertising and marketing. Give them good value and they will continue to reward you with their dollars year after year. All the slick financial and marketing techniques in the world are no substitute for an army of satisfied customers. Don't ever make the mistake of thinking of buildings, computers, consultants, or even employees as your company's greatest assets. Every company's greatest assets are its customers, because without customers there is no company. It's that simple.

Here's the Secret

Have you ever noticed how some organizations prosper, with legions of new and repeat customers year after year? And yet others just can't seem to generate enough new or repeat business and eventually fall by the wayside. Just what *are* these successful businesses doing that the unsuccessful ones aren't? Well, no doubt, if you asked them, the successful owners and managers would each give you a somewhat different formula for winning and keeping customers. Yet there is one thing that they all are doing that causes customers to want to buy and to keep coming back. And that one thing is best explained with the help of the story below about the farmer and his three pigs.

If you have read one of my previous books, listened to one of my cassette programs, seen one of my videos, or attended any of my seminars, you already know that I believe in illustrating key points with quotations, anecdotes, and fables. The main reason I do that (aside from their being entertaining) is to increase the chances that you will remember and apply the point I'm trying to make. Let's face it. You can't use knowledge that you don't remember. But if you remember the quotation or the story, chances are you'll remember the lesson. In over twenty years of work as a professional communicator, it's the single greatest teaching tool I have found and I will spare no effort to find the best way to make my point. Here is a story that illustrates the very foundation of the Greatest Business Secret in the World. And I think it's one that you will likely remember.

Once upon a time, a farmer wanted to breed his three female pigs. He loaded the sows into the back of his pickup truck and took them to visit several boars at a nearby farm. While the pigs were getting acquainted, the first farmer asked the second, "How will I know if my pigs are pregnant?"

"That's easy," said the second farmer. "They wallow in the grass when it takes and they wallow in the mud when it doesn't take."

The next morning the farmer awoke, looked out the window and found his pigs wallowing in the mud. So he loaded them into the truck and took them back to the boars. But the following morning the pigs were still wallowing in the mud. Undaunted, the farmer once again loaded the pigs into the truck and took them back to the boars for a third time, hoping for some positive results.

The following morning the farmer was away from the farm, so he anxiously phoned his wife and asked, "Are they wallowing in the grass or the mud?"

"Neither," replied the farmer's wife. "Two of them are in the back of the pickup and the third one's up front blowing the horn!"

Lest you jump to any wrong conclusions about how I want you to treat your customers, here are two basic lessons that the story teaches. And these basic lessons apply to all living creatures, including people:

- Every behavior has consequences. The female pigs visited the boars (the behavior) and liked it (the consequences).
- Future behavior depends largely on the consequences of past and present behavior. If the consequences are rewarding, the odds are great that the behavior will be repeated. The pigs' visit to the boars had very rewarding consequences so they were eager to repeat it.

To put it simply, you get more of the behavior you reward. But what does all of this have to do with customers? Plenty, and to prove my point, let's apply those two lessons to where you work:

- When a customer or potential customer visits, buys, telephones, or has some contact with your business, he will experience certain consequences of his action.
- His future behavior—that is, whether he continues to visit, buy, telephone, or have contact with your business—depends largely on those consequences. The more the customer feels rewarded, the greater the odds are that he will continue to be your customer. The less he is rewarded, the greater the odds that he will not repeat his behavior—he will become someone else's customer and spend his dollars elsewhere.

In short, winning and keeping customers depends on rewarding people for being customers. Whether they are aware of it or not, that's the one thing that all successful customer-driven businesses do. Fancy sales pitches, high-powered market strategies, and clever advertising can be very important attention-getters. And they may persuade people to become your customer. But keeping customers for any period of time depends on how well you reward them. Furthermore, it's the rewarded customer who tells others just how wonderful your products and services are, which in turn creates more customers. All of which can be summarized as the Greatest Business Secret in the World.

The rewarded customer buys, multiplies, and comes back.

You're probably wondering why I chose to call such an obvious principle "the Greatest Business Secret in the World." Well, it's greatest because it's the fundamental principle that makes success in business possible. If you doubt that, try starting a business that doesn't reward customers and see how long it takes you to make a profit.

Why do I call it a secret? Let me begin answering that question with another question: Have you been a customer lately? The sad truth is that quality service stands out today because it's so rare. Many of us are apparently unaware that our very livelihood depends on rewarding the customer. As one lady remarked to a rude clerk, "I believe you have things backward. You are overhead. I am profit." That's one reason I call it a secret.

But if you still doubt that it's a secret, try this: Ask one hundred people who work for a living, "What do you think is the single most important ingredient to success in business?" Not one in ten will say anything about customers. Yet customers are paying the wages of those very same people. In the final analysis, the customer is the real boss. Management may allocate the money but the customer determines how much there is. And the more he is rewarded, the better it flows.

How Did It Get to Be a Secret?

We can only speculate why something so simple and obvious is so often ignored and forgotten. Perhaps Thor Heyerdahl puts his finger on the problem when he said, "Progress is man's ability to complicate simplicity." In the shuffle of complex businesses and daily activities it's easy to lose sight of the customer who makes it all possible.

But my favorite explanation of how customers get forgotten comes from Dan Scoggin, president of TGI Friday's, Inc. In case you aren't familiar with the company, TGI Friday's is a chain of outstanding bistro-type restaurants and one of the best and most consistent examples of quality customer service that I know of. According to Scoggin, the problem is caused by what he has most appropriately labeled the Success Syndrome. It's a malady that sooner or later attacks almost every business and, if not corrected, goes through three predictable stages.

Stage One: You open the doors for the first time and everyone is scared. What if this goes belly up? You and your employees have mouths to feed and mortgages to pay. Failure is simply out of the question and you can't do too much to please any customer who comes in the door. If they want you to stand on your head and spit quarters, you'll try. All efforts are focused on rewarding the customer. And rewarded he is.

Stage Two: The business is open for several months and your efforts to reward customers are paying off handsomely with a steady and growing number of them. You start to feel confident as you have more business than you can handle. You were a little short with that last customer, but it's no big deal. Customers are like buses: They come along regularly and often. There are plenty more where that last one came from. The Success Syndrome has taken hold.

Stage Three: Your quality of service and performance has slipped and you're the last one to know. Sales begin to plummet and the customers just aren't coming back. You try to blame it on the competition, the economy, the weather, and anything else you can think of instead of looking within your operation where the real problems lie. Meanwhile, you try to save money by laying off a few employees and producing a cheaper product. You rationalize that customers won't know the difference, but their numbers get even smaller. As a last-ditch effort you go for broke with flashy signs, expensive advertising, and cut-rate specials to lure all those customers back, but it doesn't work. As Yogi Berra put it, "If people don't want to come out to the ball park, nobody's gonna stop 'em." Left uncorrected, this final stage is terminal.

Scoggin discovered the Success Syndrome in 1975 when TGI Friday's opened seven restaurants to overflowing crowds, with people lined up outside the doors. Yet within six months, sales at these restaurants dropped 50 percent. But when the right action was taken, it took less than six months to restore sales to their original, high level. In every case, the malady was cured by looking within each individual restaurant for specific problems and trying to view the business through the customer's eyes. Is the place clean and presentable? Are the employees helpful and friendly? To insure that the customer's viewpoint is understood, every manager must periodically sit at every table in his or her restaurant. Today, TGI Friday's has an extensive list of potential problem areas to check in a restaurant whenever sales slump. Everything from a burned-out light bulb to a waiter's bad attitude is on the list. By the time the manager gets to the end of the list, sales have bounced back.

The Success Syndrome is a silent malady. You may not feel the symptoms but you'll certainly notice the effects. The best medicine is to remember that it can strike any business almost any time, and to be constantly on guard for its symptoms. The earlier it's detected, the quicker and easier is the cure. And the cure is found by looking and taking corrective action within the business. In this case, the best vision is insight.

When we think of success in business, most of us think in terms of dollars, cents, statistics, facts, and figures. Yet all those measures of success are determined by the *behavior* of customers and the employees who serve them. Reward customers and you'll create and keep them. Fail to reward customers and you're out of business. That's the Greatest Business Secret in the World. So simple. So obvious. And so ignored.

2
BETTER THAN SELLING

The trouble with this world is that too many
people try to go through life with a catcher's mitt
on both hands.

—KENT RUTH

In the next few pages, I am going to tell you about a money-making
principle that works better than selling. You may already be using
it, and if you are, then you'll know that I am telling the truth. But
before I tell you the principle and show you how to put it to work,
here's a true story about someone who practices it.

Some years ago, after the publication of my first book, *Working
Smart,* I was hired as a spokesperson to do a series of radio and
television commercials for Pacific-Northwest Bell Telephone Company. Wanting to look my best, I went shopping for a new suit at a
suburban New Orleans clothiers near my home. As I walked in the
door I had the good fortune to meet Fred Aubert, a clothing salesman. I introduced myself, told Fred what I was looking for, and
asked for his help. He was so helpful that I have been his loyal
customer ever since.

The first thing Fred did was listen to me. He asked questions
about the commercial and requested a copy of my book so he could
get a good idea of the type of image that I would want to project on
camera. After learning more about what I needed for this particular
project, he recommended a beautiful navy-blue pin-striped suit,
which he custom fitted to my measurements. I bought the suit and
thought I was all set for the commercial.

But then I received word that the set for the commercial would have a dark background and that a dark suit was out of the question. So I went back to Fred looking for a gray suit. He offered to take back the blue one but it looked so good that I wasn't about to part with it. There were plenty of gray suits in stock but none of them seemed to fill the bill. But instead of trying to sell me one of them, Fred recommended that I try one of his competitors, where I found just the right suit. That may have cost Fred a sale, but by helping me solve my problem, he earned my loyalty.

On numerous other occasions Fred has been equally helpful. Once I was admiring a beautiful and expensive suit and had an important speaking engagement the next month. I wanted to buy the suit but Fred said, "Why don't you hold off for two weeks. We're having a sale and you might get a break on the price." I came back two weeks later and bought the suit for half price.

On other occasions Fred will call when he has something that he thinks I might be interested in and puts it aside until I can get in and take a look at it. And he is so good at fitting suits that I have taken suits that I bought overseas to him for tailoring. Whenever I go into the store, Fred has several loyal customers waiting to see him and they all get the same fine treatment that I do.

Not surprisingly, Fred is one of the top clothing salespesons in the world and has been written about in *Fortune* magazine as such. For a decade he has been the top volume salesperson in the nation for Hartmarx clothing and in one year brought in more than twice the revenue of anyone else in the three-hundred-store Hartmarx chain. What's Fred's secret?

Three Important Points

Fred has no secret formula for his success. But his approach to doing business is an excellent example of three key points that all of us in business need to know and understand.

1. The most important goal of any employee, including salespersons, is to create and keep customers. Many people, including salespersons and their managers, believe that the salesperson's primary job is to make sales. And without a doubt, making the sale is important. But making sales creates short-term dollars, while creating customers makes long- and short-term dollars. Which would you rather have?

In Fred's case, he focuses more on keeping customers satisfied than on making the sale. He could have sold me that expensive suit for full price and doubled his commission. But he has the foresight to know that he will come out better in the long run by giving the customer every possible advantage.

2. *There's a big difference between selling and helping people to buy.* It's not just a play on words. The difference is one of attitude. Traditional selling is manipulative. It takes the approach of, "Let's take what we have and talk somebody into buying it."

On the other hand, helping people to buy takes an approach of, "Let's find out what the customer wants or needs and see if we can match it with what we have. If we don't have it, maybe we can order it or make it. If not, let's send him to someone who can help and ask to serve him in the future." This approach is much less stressful for both the buyer and the seller. And there's no doubt about which approach the customer prefers.

Fred is an excellent example of someone who believes in helping people to buy. Sure, he could have talked me into buying one of his gray suits. He had plenty of them. But he didn't want me to leave the store with something that wasn't quite what I needed and sent me to one of his competitors instead. Since that time I have bought no other suits from Fred's competitor but I have bought many, many more from Fred. Selling creates a sale. Helping people to buy creates customers.

3. *People love to buy but hate to be sold.* Think about that beautiful new car the first day you brought it home. Did someone sell it to you? No, you bought it and you were proud of it. Or what about that home you built and moved into after years of planning, sacrificing, and saving. Did someone sell you that? No, you bought it and loved every minute of it. Going to the act of sale was a real triumph and a high point in your life. People love to own, to acquire, and yes, to spend money. It makes us feel important and successful.

But let's assume that new car turns out to be a real lemon with repeated maintenance headaches. Or let's assume that new house turns out to be a haven for termites, with broken pipes and a roof that leaks like someone shot a cannonball through it. Did you still buy that house or car? No, some fast-talking, silver-tongued con artist sold you a bill of goods. You didn't buy it, did you? We gladly take all the credit for the purchase we are proudest of, but are quick to blame the seller when we feel short-changed. Like it or not, it's human nature.

Did Fred sell me those beautiful suits? If you asked Fred, he would likely say, "No, Michael bought them, and doesn't he look great in them?" You see, Fred is smart enough to know that people love to buy clothes that make them look and feel their best. And if he helps them to do that, the sales will take care of themselves. He doesn't need fifty great openings or a hundred sure-fire closing techniques. His well-dressed customers bring him more business than all the fancy sales pitches in the world. When someone wants to buy a suit, whom do you think I recommend?

The Better Than Selling Principle

When I ask college seniors and graduate students majoring in business, "How many of you are interested in a career in selling?" very few hands go up. But when I ask, "How many of you studied business because you want to make a lot of money?" just about all hands go up. Why would so many people who want to make a lot of money pass up the highest-paying profession in the world? It's simple. They think of selling as a stressful, unpleasant, manipulative, arm-twisting activity and want no part of it. Few if any of us enjoy forcing products and services on people who neither want nor need them. But practically all of us find it enjoyable and personally gratifying to help others get what they need or want. And that is precisely what the better than selling principle is all about. Instead of worrying about what you make, or sell, or do for a living:

Focus on what customers want and need, help them to buy what's best for them, and make them feel good about it.

This principle is important for everyone who works and not just those in sales. You may work in a warehouse, in a laboratory, or on a production line and rarely, if ever, see one of your customers. But that customer is paying your salary, and anything you can do to improve your company's products and services is contributing to the future of your own livelihood.

Harry Bullis, a former chairman of the board of General Mills, urged his salespeople to forget about selling and concentrate on rendering service. As Bullis put it, "If you would start out each morning with the thought, 'I want to help as many people as possible today,' instead of, 'I want to make as many sales as possible today,' you would find a more easy and open approach to your buyers and make more sales. He who goes out to help his fellow man to a happier and easier way of life is exercising the highest type of salesmanship."

Ironically, the better than selling principle turns out to be the most powerful selling principle of all. It's tough to resist someone who sincerely wants to help you. But all of us, regardless of occupation, can benefit immensely by answering the question, "How can I be of greater help to our customers?" In the final analysis, you get what you give in life and that's truer in business than anyplace else. Sooner or later, the money and satisfaction you receive will be proportional to the service you render to others. Sometimes you will give more and sometimes you'll receive more. But sooner or later the scales will balance. You may have heard that expressed somewhere else as, "As ye sow, so ye shall reap."

Make helping the customer the top priority in your job. Sales and production quotas and standards are important, but they are only a means to an end. And that ultimate end is to create and keep customers. Take a few minutes at the start of each work day and ask yourself, *"How can I be of greater help to my customers?"* Keep a diary handy and whenever you have a new idea, write it down and resolve to start using it. Encourage others where you work to do the same thing. Make it a contest and give prizes to those who come up with the best new ideas for helping customers. In fact, brainstorming as many answers to the question as possible in a fun atmosphere makes a great group problem-solving exercise.

Someone once noted that business is a lot like tennis—those who don't serve well end up losing. Try the better than selling principle in your job for one year and you'll never do business any other way. Even if you don't make more money (which is very unlikely), you will feel so much better about yourself that you'll make it a habit.

3

THE GREATEST CUSTOMER YOU'LL EVER WIN

To love what you do and feel that it matters—how could anything be more fun?

—KATHARINE GRAHAM

The famous New York diamond dealer Harry Winston heard about a wealthy Dutch merchant who was looking for a certain kind of diamond to add to his collection. Winston called the merchant, told him that he thought he had the perfect stone, and invited the collector to come to New York and examine it.

The collector flew to New York and Winston assigned a salesman to meet him and show the diamond. When the salesman presented the diamond to the merchant he described the expensive stone by pointing out all of its fine technical features. The merchant listened and praised the stone but turned away and said, "It's a wonderful stone but not exactly what I want."

Winston, who had been watching the presentation from a distance, stopped the merchant going out the door and asked, "Do you mind if I show you that diamond once more?" The merchant agreed and Winston presented the stone. But instead of talking about the technical features of the stone, Winston spoke spontaneously about his own genuine admiration of the diamond and what a rare thing of beauty it was. Abruptly, the customer changed his mind and bought the diamond.

While he was waiting for the diamond to be packaged and

brought to him, the merchant turned to Winston and asked, "Why did I buy it from you when I had no difficulty saying no to your salesman?"

Winston replied, "That salesman is one of the best men in the business and he knows more about diamonds than I do. I pay him a good salary for what he knows. But I would gladly pay him twice as much if I could put into him something that I have and he lacks. You see, he *knows* diamonds, but I *love* them."

That story illustrates one of the single greatest principles of persuasion: **People are far more persuaded by the depths of your beliefs and emotions than any amount of logic or knowledge you possess.**

People don't care how much you know until they know how much you care about: 1) your products and services and 2) them. There is absolutely no substitute for an honest, unshakable, enthusiastic belief that the products and services your business offers are the best available anywhere. Couple this with a sincere passion for helping people and you have an unbeatable combination for creating and keeping customers. And that's why:

The greatest customer you'll ever win is you!

To put it another way, the greatest sale you will ever make is made the day that you buy your own product. Being totally sold on the value of what you have to offer automatically makes you a super salesperson. Cavett Robert, founder of the National Speakers Association, expressed this idea beautifully. Pointing first to his head and then to his heart, Cavett said, "You tell from here but you sell from here. The most persuasive person in the world is the one who has a fanatical belief in an idea, a product, or a service. Words can be refused. But a positive attitude that springs from a sincere belief cannot."

People are persuaded more by attitude than logic for two basic reasons that you should always keep in mind as you deal with customers or with people in general:

- People are ruled by their emotions
- Emotions are contagious

For years you have been taught that human beings are intelligent, rational creatures. You've been taught that our ability to reason sets us apart from all other living beings. You went to school for years to learn how to think intelligently, logically, and objectively. And now, Michael LeBoeuf has the nerve to tell you that people are governed by their emotions? You better believe it!

Without a doubt, humans are the most rational of living beings. But that doesn't mean that most of our decisions are based on logic. The plain fact is that we base nearly all of our choices on how we *feel* about a situation. And then we justify those emotional choices to ourselves and others with logic. Look at whom we marry, the foods we eat, the kind of clothes we wear, where we live, our choice of careers, and it becomes very apparent just how much we are ruled by our emotions. We all live at the feelings level, and those feelings call the shots. (More about this in the next chapter.)

But in addition to being all-powerful, emotions are highly contagious. Helena Modjeska, a nineteenth-century actress, was extremely popular because of her ability to communicate her emotions. She once gave a dramatic reading in Polish (her native tongue) to an English-speaking audience and had them in tears when she finished. Little did they know that the content of Helena's message was the reciting of the Polish alphabet!

What do you do when someone you're with yawns? That's right, you yawn. Play a recording of someone continuously laughing to another person and chances are that person will also start laughing. Watch a sad movie and the tears will start to flow. Feelings are highly transferable and those who know how to do it rule the world.

Ronald Reagan is a case in point. While you may or may not agree with his politics, there is no denying his persuasive powers. He is a super salesman extraordinaire. What's his secret? Some have called him the great communicator, the Teflon president, and attributed his success to his theatrical ability. But at the core of Reagan's persuasive prowess lies his unswerving, deep-seated belief that his policies are right for America and the world. And that, in a nutshell, is why he is so persuasive. His sincerity communicates and transfers his beliefs and emotions to others because the best salesperson is the true believer.

The World Is Your Mirror and Your Mind Is a Magnet

A salesperson remarks, "I know this sounds strange, but I just knew that Williams was going to buy that ring the minute he walked into the store. Do you think it was clairvoyance or mental telepathy?" No, it wasn't ESP, clairvoyance, or any other hocus-pocus. The salesperson had already made the sale in his own mind before talking to the customer. His expectation that the sale was going to happen gave him an almost hypnotic persuasive power. His own belief generated an excitement that was transferred to the customer. And the customer bought.

At another store earlier that same morning, another salesperson says, "I can't explain why, but I could tell that Williams really wasn't interested in buying a ring." Of course Williams wasn't interested. The salesperson didn't believe he was going to make a sale and his negative expectation generated negative results. There was no positive expectation, no enthusiasm to transfer to the customer, and no sale.

Obviously, there's much more to creating and keeping customers than simply believing in your products and services and believing that everyone is going to buy them. But keep this point in mind: Your world is a mirror and your mind is a magnet. What you perceive in this world is largely a reflection of your own attitudes and beliefs. And life will give you what you attract with your thoughts. Think, act, and talk negatively and your world will likely be negative. Think, act, and talk with enthusiasm and you will attract positive results. In short, you won't always get what you want, but in the long run you'll get what you expect. When you sincerely believe you're offering the customer something of true value, odds are that the customer will see it as such. In the final analysis, persuasion isn't converting people to your way of thinking. It's converting people to your way of *feeling* and *believing*.

If you know what you're doing, love what you're doing, and believe in what you're doing, you'll be totally sold on the products and services you offer. And that's the greatest customer you'll ever win.

4

THE ONLY TWO THINGS PEOPLE EVER BUY

There is no such thing as a commodity.

—THEODORE LEVITT, professor, Harvard Business School

Have you ever stopped and asked yourself, "What are our customers really buying when they do business with us?" While it may seem like a dumb question at first, I can assure you that it's one of the most important questions that every employee from the chairman of the board to the man on the assembly line needs to know the answer to. And the answer is not as obvious as you may think. You see, customers don't buy what your company sells. Instead, they buy what those goods and services do for them. To illustrate, consider the following plea from an anonymous customer:

Don't sell me clothes. Sell me a sharp appearance, style, and attractiveness.

Don't sell me insurance. Sell me peace of mind and a great future for my family and me.

Don't sell me a house. Sell me comfort, contentment, a good investment, and pride of ownership.

Don't sell me books. Sell me pleasant hours and the profits of knowledge.

Don't sell me toys. Sell my children happy moments.

Don't sell me a computer. Sell me the pleasures and profits of the miracles of modern technology.

Don't sell me tires. Sell me freedom from worry and low cost per mile.

Don't sell me airline tickets. Sell me a fast, safe, on-time arrival at my destination feeling like a million dollars.

Don't sell me *things*. Sell me ideals, feelings, self-respect, home life, and happiness.

Please don't sell me *things*.

Despite all of the untold millions of products and services for sale in today's market place, customers will exchange their hard-earned money for only two things:

• Good feelings
• Solutions to problems

In the final analysis, the success or failure of any business depends on how many people it rewards with those two things and how well it does it. As Francis (Buck) Rodgers, a former vice-president of marketing for IBM, put it, "The secret is to understand the customer's problems and provide solutions so as to help that customer be profitable and feel good about the transaction."

A Crash Course in Customer Behavior

If customers buy good feelings and solutions, then it's your job to know how to provide them. And that, in turn, means understanding more about the feelings customers have and how they go about making a decision to buy. Earlier I mentioned that people are ruled by their emotions and emotions are contagious. Now, let's expand on those two concepts and apply them to customers.

The first important point to remember is that **people buy emotionally and justify with logic.** In the overwhelming majority of cases we don't buy what we need. We buy what we want and wants are based on feelings. For example, you *need* food but you *want* a steak for dinner tonight. You need transportation to work but you want that new sports car you saw in the dealer's showroom yesterday. And once you decide that you really want it, you'll think up all sorts of logical reasons for buying it, such as, "It gets good mileage, it's easy to park, and the dealer threw in an extra year's warranty to make it a super buy." So you buy it and convince yourself that it was a sound, logical business decision. But that's not the real reason that you bought it. You bought it because it makes you feel like a free spirit after being caged in an office all day. You bought it because you'll feel great when you get admiring looks from members of the opposite sex as you drive around town with the top down. You bought it because all the gauges and high-tech bells and whistles at your command make you feel important, up-to-date, and in step with the future. In short, you bought it because it makes you feel good. It's feelings and not logic that cause people to buy the overwhelming majority of the time.

THE FOUR EMOTIONAL STATES

According to psychologists, a person is capable of experiencing only four basic emotions. Those emotions are:

- Glad
- Sad
- Mad
- Scared

Those are the only feelings we ever have, and at any given time we are in one of those four emotional states. You may ask, "What about other feelings such as love, hate, and sympathy?" Those are just special cases of the four emotional states. For example, love is a special case of glad, hate is a special case of mad, and sympathy is a special case of sad. At any given point in time a person is feeling either glad, mad, sad, or scared, and that emotional state will govern his behavior.

The main point to remember is this: *Customers only buy when they are feeling glad about you and your products and services.* If you make them mad, they will either go away or give you a hard time. But they won't buy. If you make them sad, they will go away, because people withdraw when they feel sad. If you scare them, they will most likely withdraw but they certainly won't buy. **People spend money when and where they feel good.** It's just that simple. Walt Disney realized that years ago and that's the main reason his company has been such a huge financial success.

SOLUTIONS TO PROBLEMS

A popular marketing axiom states, "People don't buy goods, they buy solutions to problems. They don't buy quarter-inch drill bits, they buy quarter-inch holes." When people buy solutions to problems, what they are actually buying is the expectation of feeling glad. If you're a customer with a problem and I solve it for you, are you going to feel glad, mad, sad, or scared? That's right, you'll feel glad.

But just what is a problem? My favorite working definition comes from Orlando, Florida, sales trainer Bill Bishop. According to Bishop, "A problem is the difference between what you have and what you want." So, if you want to solve a customer's problem, ask him, "What do you have?" (What's the situation now?) and, "What do you want?" (How would you like it to be?) Once you have the answers to those two questions, you can decide if and how you can solve the problem. But until you know the answers to those two questions, any problem-solving you do will be purely accidental.

The Right Touch

Author Tom Wolfe coined the term "the right stuff" to describe that special, undefinable quality that our pioneer astronauts possessed. Just as the right stuff makes for good astronauts, the right touch is what it takes to win and keep customers. Your company may sell the finest products and services in the marketplace, but it's how customers *feel* about your products and services that ultimately determine how successful your business will be. If they feel good, they'll buy and come back. If they don't, they won't. With that thought in mind, here are some key ideas you can use to put the right touch to work where you work.

1. Put yourself in the glad emotional state. Remember, people buy when they feel glad and feelings are contagious. Be the carrier and not the catcher. People like to do business when and where they feel good.

You may be thinking, "I don't always feel glad at work. Sometimes I feel mad, sad, or scared. What do I do then?" Well here is a technique you can use to help yourself feel glad:

Act the way you want to feel and soon you'll feel the way you act.

Most of us know that actions follow emotions. We feel a certain way and that feeling governs our behavior. But it's also true that emotions follow actions. So, if you want to feel glad, act glad.

Try this: The next time you feel sad, mad, or scared, go look at yourself in a mirror and start smiling. I'm not talking about a false, paste-on smile, but a genuine smile that starts with the corners of your eyes. Do it for several minutes and you will actually start to feel better, because emotions follow actions.

And here's another technique for staying glad. When things go wrong remember that things almost always seem more important in the present than they actually are. The present tends to make us nearsighted unless we recognize and adjust our thinking to compensate for it. Ask yourself, "How important will this be next month or next year?" Most of the time it won't be very important at all. An old saying has it that elephants don't bite. It's the fleas that drive you crazy if you let them. Stay happy. It's good for business and good for your health.

2. Never tell customers your problems. Ninety percent of them don't care and the rest will actually be glad that you're as miserable as they are. Telling people your problems makes them sad and sad people only buy at funeral homes. If you want to run customers off, just keep telling them bad news. As Isaac Singer put it, "If you keep on saying that things are going to be bad, you have a good chance of being a prophet."

Despite what you read, see, or hear in the media, life isn't easy for anybody. We all have our share of problems and discussing them provides a healthy emotional outlet—but not with customers.

Similarly, encourage customers to tell you only about problems that you can solve for them. Don't greet them with, "How are you?" That's inviting an answer like, "How am I? I'll tell you how I am. My teenage daughter is pregnant, my son got busted for drugs, the IRS just seized my bank account, and my spouse ran off with my business partner and took all the money." All of which will put them in the sad emotional state and they will leave your business feeling worse for the experience. Instead, be upbeat and greet them with, "It's good to meet you," or "Glad to see you again."

3. Remember that customers buy for their reasons, not ours. To quote George Bernard Shaw, "It is unwise to do unto others as you would have them do unto you. Their tastes may not be the same."

Every customer has a different emotional makeup and different problems that need to be solved. You win and keep customers by giving them what they want and not what you think they should want.

About 75 percent of all buying decisions are based on unconscious needs and wants, such as prestige, habit, or perceived value, and on a multitude of other biases. Of course, few customers will admit or even be aware that they are responding to emotional and unconscious reasons for buying. Your basic job is to size up and respond to each customer's wants and problems in a way that makes him feel glad. For example, does he want a bargain? Explain why your products and services are the best deal for the money. Does he want to feel important? Recognize his importance and praise his wisdom for considering your products and services. (Two groups of people always fall for flattery: men and women.) Is he afraid of making a mistake? Give him testimonials, names of satisfied customers to contact, and a no-risk money-back guarantee.

If you feel a customer is making a decision that he may later regret, politely tell him, explain your reasons and then back off. It's his money and his choice. Don't ever tell him he is wrong. You'll just make him mad, and mad customers don't buy or come back.

4. *Act as if you are the only personal contact that the customer has with the company and behave as if the entire company's image depends on you.* That's what IBM encourages its employees to do, and its record for outstanding customer service speaks for itself. When you are dealing with a customer, you are the company to that customer, and his decision to become or remain a customer depends on you.

5. *Use both logic and emotion to win and keep customers.* While the overwhelming majority of buying decisions are made emotionally, never underestimate the importance of logic. Emotion causes customers to buy but logic keeps them sold and coming back. Have you ever gotten excited about a product, bought it on the spot, and regretted it later? That's called post-decision remorse and it's bad for business. Customers who suffer post-decision remorse walk out the door feeling glad and wake up tomorrow feeling mad, sad, or scared. If they come back, it won't be to buy.

You prevent post-decision remorse by giving customers sound, logical reasons that your products and services are a good value for the money. Once a customer wants to buy, he needs reasons justifying the purchase and in effect is saying, "Please give me some reasons so I won't regret this later." Your job is to point out the logical benefits of what he is getting for his money and see to it that he gets them.

6. *Use the problem-solving approach to move customers from mad, sad, or scared to glad.* Whenever a customer has a problem calmly ask him, "What is the situation now?" and "What would you like it to be?" Once you know the answers to these two questions, you can decide how to solve his problem. Even if you can't solve his problem, letting him express it and taking the time to listen will make him feel better. Just knowing that you cared enough to listen and tried to help will leave him with a much better impression than if you had taken a "that's-not-my-problem" attitude.

In summary, the degree of success of any business hinges on how many people it rewards with good feelings and solutions to problems and how well it does both. What good feelings and solutions does your business provide? How do you help your company give them? And what can you do to provide more good feelings and solutions for the customer? Those are three important questions whose answers can be found only by focusing on the customer and what your business can do for him. Master merchant Stanley Marcus put it this way: "If you pay attention to the customers they come back, and if you pay attention to the goods, they don't come back." That one idea is worth more than any item in a Neiman-Marcus catalog. Put it to work and you'll see what I mean.

5

THEY'LL BUY MUCH MORE WHEN THEY BUY YOU

Charm is the quality in others that makes us more
satisfied with ourselves.

—HENRI FREDERIC AMIEL

How customers feel about the people that serve or sell them is a key
factor in winning and keeping them. Think about it. Don't you
judge a service station by the attendant who fills your tank or a bank
by the teller who waits on you?

I recently switched dry cleaners because I got tired of dealing with
the dim bulbs who waited on me. They did good work but the clerks
would drag themselves out of the back looking semicomatose and
say, "M'ep ya?" (It was too much trouble to say, "May I help
you?") And when I went to pick up my clothes, they took what
seemed like an eternity to find them, collected the money, and
closed the transaction with a monotone, "Ank ya." After a few
times, I started to wonder if they were drinking or sniffing the dry-
cleaning fluid. They treated every customer I observed the same
way, and gave me the same moribund routine every time I did
business with them. So now I take my dry cleaning down the street.

On the other hand, I recently switched pest control services for
just the opposite reason. For the past eleven years, Emile, a pest
control technician, has kept the creepy crawlers out of my home. He
comes by once a month to spray the house and yard and I always
look forward to his visits because he goes out of his way to be

friendly. He asks about what I'm writing, where I have been speaking, how I like my new car, and so forth. We also talk about what he has been up to and some of the interesting places he visits as he makes his rounds.

A lot of people would say Emile wastes too much time talking to customers rather than doing his job. But taking the time to be nice to customers paid off handsomely for Emile last year. It seems that Emile and his former boss had a disagreement that resulted in the boss firing both Emile and Emile's wife, who worked as the boss's secretary. But did Emile fall on hard times? Not at all. He started his own pest control service and took approximately 115 of his 120 customers with him. Furthermore, Emile was the only technician that his former boss had. Consequently, the boss suddenly found himself the owner of a pest control business with practically no customers. You can bet that bugged him.

In any business, the people who deal directly with the customers can make or break the business. Make a good impression and the customer buys, multiplies, and comes back. Make a poor impression and you run him off. It's as simple as that. And the more service-oriented the business is, the more crucial it becomes to have front-line people who know how to sell themselves.

To be sure, selling yourself to a customer (or anyone else) is an art that must be tailored to your own personality, the customer, and the situation. Yet there is one underlying strategy whose application will almost always guarantee that you'll make a good impression. Here it is:

Help them to like themselves better and they'll love you.

Jane, recently married, was having lunch with a friend and explaining why she married Bill instead of Bob. "Bob is Mr. Everything." Jane said. "He's handsome, well educated, extremely intelligent, clever, and has a very successful career. In fact, when I was with Bob I felt like I was with the most wonderful person in the world."

"Then why did you marry Bill?" her friend asked.

Jane replied, "Because when I'm with Bill, I feel like *I'm* the most wonderful person in the world."

That story illustrates the single most important key to selling yourself. This isn't to say that other factors, such as looking your best and being well mannered, aren't important, because they are.

But the most effective way to make a positive and lasting impression is to concentrate on boosting the customer's self-image.

Each of us has a self-image that serves as our main contact with reality, and its preservation and confirmation is the single greatest reason that we do the things we do. We tenaciously cling to both the good and bad parts of our self-image. Believe that you are shy, friendly, lazy, important, aggressive, or whatever and you will tend to behave that way. For better or worse we are attracted to people and situations that confirm what we believe or want to believe to be true about ourselves. And if you want to make people sad, mad, or scared, just try threatening their self-image.

For example, I fancy myself a good writer. That's part of my self-image. If you sincerely compliment me about something you learned or enjoyed from reading one of my books, you're confirming a positive part of my self-image and I will like you better for it. But let's suppose you read one of my books and tell me, "Michael, when are you going to learn how to write? Your disorganized, purple prose makes it impossible for me to make any sense out of what you're trying to say." Do you really think that I'll look forward to seeing you again? Not on your life! You threatened my self-image and said, in effect, "Michael, you aren't who you think you are." The strongest force in life isn't self-preservation—it's preservation of self-image. The next time you feel insulted or angry at something someone says, ask yourself, "Is it because my self-image is being attacked?" Chances are the answer will be "yes."

Every customer you meet wants and needs to have his self-image confirmed and boosted. Focus on building the customer's self-image and you're well on your way to selling yourself. Most people don't do this. They get so wrapped up in trying to impress the customer with their products, services, or themselves, that they forget about the customer and his needs. And as Kaye Halverson and Karen Hess wrote, "If you're all wrapped up in yourself, you are over-dressed."

There are numerous ways you can go about boosting a customer's self-image, and we will get to the specifics shortly. But first, here is another strategy to help you toward that end:

Open an emotional bank account with each customer.

Management consultant Steven Covey has come up with an interesting way of viewing human relationships. According to Covey, with each new relationship we open what could be called an emotional bank account to which we can make deposits and from which we can make withdrawals. When we help others to get what they want and feel better about themselves we are making a deposit that will likely pay big dividends in the future. But when we call on others to help us, or make them feel worse, we are making a withdrawal, and with too many withdrawals we run the risk of becoming overdrawn and losing the account. The one major difference between financial and emotional bank accounts is that an emotional bank account usually requires continual small deposits in order to maintain its present balance. It's an interesting and useful concept for understanding how to make any type of relationship grow and prosper, be it parent-child, husband-wife, boss-subordinate, or employee-customer.

Every time you boost a customer's self-image you make a significant deposit to the emotional bank account and increase the odds of winning and keeping him. Here are five specific ideas to help you toward that end.

1. Develop a genuine interest in and admiration for your customers. To quote IBM founder Thomas Watson, "If you don't genuinely like your customers, the chances are they won't buy." The more you know and admire about the customers the easier it is to make deposits to the emotional bank account in a way that's meaningful to them. Get them to talk about themselves and listen with your undivided attention. A good rule of thumb is to let them do 80 percent of the talking. People are much more likely to buy when they're talking than when you're talking. As Dr. William King noted, "A gossip is one who talks to you about other people. A bore is one who talks to you about himself. And a brilliant conversationalist is one who talks to you about yourself."

2. Recognize and praise people for what they want to be recognized and praised for. With a little observation and common sense it's easy to spot what people want to be complimented for. If you notice that a customer has lost weight, has a suntan, or has a new hair style, acknowledge and compliment it. Is the customer wearing a special-looking pin or piece of jewelry? It may be an award or have special significance. Ask about it. Is there a photograph on his desk or a diploma or certificate hanging on his wall? Ask about it. He must be proud of it or he wouldn't be displaying it. Did he just buy a new possession that he's proud of? Tell him how fortunate he is. Tact is the art of seeing people as they wish to be seen.

Two main points need to be stressed about the art of giving compliments. The first is that they must be sincere. People know when they are being conned, and insincere flattery is a good way to run off a customer. Second, make them specific. Don't tell Mrs. Johnson that you like her new tan and leave it at that. Tell her it makes her look ten years younger or ten pounds lighter, or that it brings out the best in her.

One final important point about compliments. If possible, find a way to compliment the customer for something that results from having used your products and services in the past. If your business helps him solve important problems or saves him time or money, point out how doing business with your company is a smart move on his part. Compliment him on being intelligent enough to take advantage of the benefits your business offers.

3. Put them at ease and establish rapport. We all prefer the company of people who make us feel accepted and relaxed. Have you ever wondered why some people are more comfortable to be with than others? Well, so have a lot of behavioral scientists, and they have discovered a number of specific kinds of behavior that contribute to establishing a personal rapport. Here are several that anyone can practice.

- Smile sincerely—not a false, paste-on smile, but one that starts with your eyes.
- Keep a relaxed, open stance.
- Lean slightly toward the customer, being careful not to invade his personal space.
- Maintain eye contact. You will be considered more confident, honest, and knowledgeable by customers.
- Occasionally touch the person in a nonthreatening manner.
- Know the customer's name and use it when speaking to him.
- Subtly mirror the customer's behavior. Match his rate of breathing, speak at his rate of speech and in his tone of voice. Assume a posture similar to his and use similar body language. We all relate to those who we feel are like us.

4. Use humor where it's relevant and appropriate. Laughter is a tremendous influence tool. We all like people who make us feel good. Furthermore, we know that when people laugh they are listening and when they are listening they can be influenced. And influence is the name of the game when it comes to winning and keeping customers.

The most effective humor is brief and self-effacing. The shorter the story, the greater the impact. And telling a joke on yourself tells others that you don't take yourself too seriously and have the self-confidence to laugh at yourself. It's another great way to build rapport.

5. *Let them know that you're thinking about them.* Send your customers congratulatory cards for birthdays, promotions, graduations, or anything you can congratulate them for. Keep a list of their professional and personal interests and if you see an article that would be of interest, clip it out and send it with a brief, handwritten note. Most customers only hear from businesses when they're trying to sell them. Be different and add a personal touch. Frequent small deposits to your customers' emotional bank accounts will ultimately result in deposits that you can take to the bank.

6

THE CUSTOMER'S PERCEPTION IS EVERYTHING

People expect a certain reaction from a business and when you pleasantly exceed those expectations you've somehow passed an important psychological threshold.

—RICHARD THALHEIMER, president, The Sharper Image

Every business, regardless of size, has a reputation for the quality of goods and services it delivers. What quality of customer service do you associate with IBM, Delta Air Lines, and Disney? Pretty high, right? Now, what quality of customer service do you associate with your local water company, electric company, or the post office? Chances are you rated this group lower.

It's not that the second group fails to give good service. In fact, they give excellent service for a very reasonable price. Think about it. You can drop a letter into any corner mailbox and send it anywhere in the country for the price of a stamp. And for a nominal monthly charge, you have water and electricity at your disposal, almost always without fail. You can even make an excellent case that the latter group provides more service than the former. What would you rather give up for one month: IBM, Delta, and Disney, or running water, electricity, and mail?

Why do companies like IBM, Delta, and Disney have such an excellent customer service image? One key reason is that they do, in fact, give excellent service. But another equally important reason is that they have learned the subtle art of reminding the customer of the great service they give. On the other hand, utility companies and the post office have traditionally placed less emphasis on making the customer aware that he is getting a good deal. Consequently, the customer takes the good service for granted and only thinks about the company when the lights or the water goes out, a letter gets lost, or they ask for a rate increase. When they are right we never remember, but when they're wrong we never forget. The result is a poor customer service image.

You may have the most efficient, dedicated workforce in the world. You can care more about your customers than seems humanly possible. You can stay awake at night thinking up better ways to reward and serve them. But until you make the customer aware that you're taking very special care of him and giving him his money's worth, you're wasting your time. *It's not the quality of service that you give but the quality of service that the customer perceives that causes him to buy and come back.*

What the Customer Perceives Is Reality to Him

Perception is how we make sense out of what we experience. Your interpretation of what you see and hear is just that—your interpretation. And the same is true for your customers.

Did you know that no human being ever comes into direct contact with reality? Everything we experience is the product of what our sensory devices and our nervous system manufactures. For example, consider the book you now hold in your hands. You perceive it as a rather static collection of sheets of paper, with print on the pages, surrounded by a cover. Yet scientists tell us that what you are really holding in your hands is a swarming mass of electrons. The limitations of your sensory devices, your brain, and your nervous system prevent you from perceiving the mass of electrons as electrons. Instead, the combination of your past experiences and your physical and psychological makeup tell you that you're holding a book in your hands, and that's what you perceive.

Inasmuch as no two people have the same physical and emotional makeup and past experiences, no two people perceive anything the exact same way. Yet for any one person, what he perceives is reality to him. When it comes to winning and keeping customers, it's the customer's perception of the quality of service that determines how successful your business will be. The final measure of quality customer service is simply how the customer perceives it. It's as simple as that.

Now for the big question: What causes customers to perceive service as good or bad? Here's a very important concept to remember:

Perceived service quality is the difference between what they get and what they expect.

Every customer comes with certain expectations about the quality of the goods, the services, and the total experience of dealing with your business. When you exceed his expectations he perceives the quality as relatively high. When you fail to meet his expectations he perceives the quality as relatively low. In the back of every customer's brain is a scale that compares what he gets with what he expected. And the more it comes up on the plus side, the greater will be the perceived quality of your customer service.

"Why is this so important?" you ask. It's important because relative perceived quality is the single most important factor in determining long-term profitability. That conclusion was reached by the Strategic Planning Institute of Cambridge, Massachusetts, after testing thousands of variables in numerous businesses to determine what impact various strategies have on long-term profitability. After assembling an extensive data base and doing a lot of hard research, they came to the obvious conclusion that you win and keep customers by giving them a good deal for their money *as they perceive it*. In addition, the SPI study found that businesses that rated low on service averaged a meager 1 percent return on sales and lost market share at a rate of 2 percent per year. On the other hand, companies that scored high in service averaged a 12 percent return on sales, gained market share at the rate of 6 percent per year, and charged significantly higher prices. Is that important enough?

Keys to Shaping Customer Perception

An old Malayan proverb states, "The turtle lays thousands of eggs without anyone knowing, but when the hen lays an egg, the whole country is informed." It's not enough to reward your customers with good service. You have to make them aware of the good deal they're getting for doing business with you and keep reminding them in many subtle, different ways. In reality there's no such thing as a good deal or a bad deal. Only the customer's thinking makes it so.

For example, some years ago a company that sold canned red salmon was being outsold by pink salmon ten to one. In desperation, they called in an advertising agency and said, "Do anything, as long as it's legal, to get our sales up." The agency agreed to try and in a few short months, sales skyrocketed. When the company asked the agency rep, "What on earth did you guys do?" he replied, "All we did was redesign the label on the can." The new label read, "Authentic Norwegian Red Salmon—guaranteed not to turn pink." Now, that's shaping customer perception!

Whether it's planned or not, every business has an image and the most successful have learned that a positive image doesn't just happen. It's the result of a lot of planning, hard work, and doing a number of things consistently well. Here are some essentials to shaping a high-quality service image in the customer's eyes:

1. Develop a customer profile. Get a clear picture of the kind of customers you want to win and keep. What's their age range, income level, sex, marital status, educational level, occupation, and life style? What services are most important to them? The more you can precisely define which customers you're trying to serve, the easier it is to perceive your business through their eyes. Conversely, a business that tries to be all things to all people runs the high risk of becoming nobody to everyone. If others who don't fit the profile become customers, that's great. But target your efforts for a particular segment of the market you want to reach.

2. Look at your business through your customer's eyes. And when I say *look,* I mean that literally. 85 percent of what we remember comes through our eyes, 11 percent comes through our ears, and the rest through our other senses. Have you ever noticed how clean Disneyworld is? It's no accident. Rather, it's a subtle way of building employee morale and telling the customer, "We take pride in our work."

Take a visual inventory of your operation. Start by evaluating your own appearance. Do you dress and make the effort to look like someone that your customers would come to for advice? Next, look at your facilities. Does the customer see a clean, neat, professional operation or one that looks poorly maintained? Remember, one major difference between services and manufacturing is that services are often produced in the presence of the customer. In effect, the customer is in the factory and anything that he sees has a tremendous influence on shaping his perception.

Next, evaluate all communication that customers receive from you. Are your business cards, stationery, and printed materials crisp, professional, and neat? Are letters neatly typed and free of grammatical and spelling errors? Telephone your place of business posing as a customer and see how you get treated. Is this the kind of operation where you would like to spend your hard-earned dollars or can you think of some other place that would give you a better deal? Every single contact the customer has with your business is shaping his perception for better or worse.

3. *Beware of overpromising and building unrealistic expectations.* It may make you a sale but will likely cost you customers. The higher you build customer expectations, the harder it becomes to meet and exceed them. You run the high risk of customers feeling short-changed, not coming back and telling others. It's a sure road to a bad image. If you think you can finish the job in three days, promise it in five. If you have to give the customer an estimated cost, it's better to err on the high side and pleasantly surprise him later. Similarly, be sure you can deliver a new service flawlessly before marketing it. Too much newness can ruin you.

4. *Use problems as opportunities to demonstrate just what great service your company gives.* Customers judge the quality of service in two basic ways: 1) how well you deliver what you promise and 2) how you handle exceptions and problems. Most businesses treat problems like bad colds. They simply treat the bad symptoms and hope they go away. But the smart ones go that extra mile for the customer and show him just how dedicated they are to making sure that he feels good about doing business with them.

For example, consider how The Sharper Image handles its routine problems. Any item ordered from a Sharper Image catalog can be returned within thirty days of original purchase, not for credit but for a full cash refund. If you see an item that you ordered from The Sharper Image advertised at a lower price, send them the ad within thirty days of receiving your order and you'll receive a full refund or credit for the difference. If you order an item that's currently not in stock, you automatically get a 10 percent discount and they will pay the shipping. There is a toll-free 800 number for customer complaints to insure that all problems are resolved quickly and in the customer's interest. To be sure, all this costs money— about five thousand dollars per week. But consider this: Richard Thalheimer started The Sharper Image in 1979 by advertising a sports watch in *Runner's World* magazine. By 1987 annual sales of The Sharper Image topped 120 million dollars.

Similarly, IBM is noted for overkill whenever a problem arises. When a computer malfunctions at a corporation, technicians in large numbers descend with banners unfurled and profuse apologies about how sorry they are that something went wrong. Follow-up telephone calls to the customer are made before, during, and after the problem is solved to reassure the customer that his satisfaction is their top priority. Some would argue that IBM overdoes it to a fault but there's a method to their madness. They're constantly reminding the customer that they give great service, and are thereby shaping the customer's perception. Think about this: Have you ever gotten an apology from a utility when its service went out? Most people haven't, and that's probably one reason that utilities' quality of service is perceived as low.

5. Develop a unique relationship with your customers and treat each one as someone special. A customer received a statement from a computer that read, "If you fail to pay this bill within thirty days we are turning your account over to a human." Treating every customer in the same impersonal manner is one sure way to destroy a company's service image. I still get angry at the local water company when I remember getting a form letter threatening to cut off my water if I failed to pay my bill within ten days. What happened was that I was preoccupied that month and simply forgot to sit down and pay my bills. It was pure negligence on my part, but is that any way to treat a customer who's paid his water bill on time from the same residence for over ten years?

On the other hand, I was recently amazed at the personalized service that I received at the Hyatt Hotel in downtown Chicago. The desk clerk personally introduced himself, welcomed me, asked where I was from, and then personally introduced me to the bellman who showed me to my room. Both went out of their way to treat me as an individual and give numerous suggestions to make my stay more pleasant. The next morning I was waiting in a long line to check out and a young lady approached me and said, "If you have a major credit card, I can check you out in thirty seconds on one of our computerized billing machines." One minute later I was in a taxi heading to my appointment. Because of their friendly, helpful, personalized service, I left the Hyatt very favorably impressed.

Even the briefest of encounters can leave a customer with a positive impression. After being treated like livestock on a late-arriving Canadian airline, I raced to my Delta connection in Seattle with only two minutes to spare. As I rushed onto the waiting plane, gasping for breath, I said to the attendant, "Am I glad to see you!" She smilingly replied, "Well, we're glad to see you." Customers, like hearts, go where they are appreciated.

6. *Keep in touch and keep them informed.* If you fail to stay in touch with your customers, they won't be aware of the good service you're giving them until something goes wrong and they don't get it. But by staying in touch after the sale or between sales, you can remind them of the fine service you give, make them aware of new products and services, and offer information to help them get more for their money. Periodic telephone calls, personal letters, newsletters, and occasional social calls are all good vehicles for staying in touch. But by all means, stay in touch and let them know that their satisfaction is priority number 1 with both word and deed.

Similarly, educating your customers is another important key to building a quality service image. The more a customer knows about your products and services and how to use them, the easier it bcomes for him to see the value. Furthermore, an informed customer feels more in control and on top of the situation. Customer education can take many forms. Whirlpool Corporation has developed a series of pamphlets and a do-it-yourself kit to help customers service their appliances and know when to call for outside service. Neiman-Marcus employees have a thorough knowledge of each product and what makes it special so customers can make an intelligent buying decision. Crocker Bank gives its customers ideas and suggestions for reducing long waiting lines and lengthy bank transactions. If you have a necessary policy that irritates customers, tell them why it's necessary and how it benefits them. Every customer has a need to know, and the more you attend to this need, the more value he will perceive.

7. *Remember that a large part of good service is show biz.* A man eating in an Italian restaurant in the United States told the owner,

"Your veal parmigiana is better than the one I had in Italy last month." The owner replied, "Of course it is. You see, they use domestic cheese. Ours is imported." An important part of any service job is to entertain, amuse, and make the customer feel good in as many ways as possible. For example, one survey revealed that two out of three women choose hairdressers on the basis of their social abilities rather than for their hair-cutting skills. In many service jobs, style is more important than ability when it comes to what the customer perceives. When you're in the presence of a customer you're on stage and the spotlight is on you. Part of doing your job well is giving a good performance when you do it.

In summary, the acid test for the success of any business is the perceived overall value that customers think they are getting. The companies that offer value consistently to their customers are the ones that win and keep them. But when perceived value disappears, so do the customers. When it comes to customers, what matters most isn't what you know or whom you know, but how you are known to them.

7

TO WIN NEW CUSTOMERS, ASK THE GOLDEN QUESTION

Genius: A person who aims at something no one else can see and hits it.

—*Bits & Pieces* magazine

If rewarding customers is the key to winning and keeping them, then it naturally follows that the surest path to more customers is to provide rewards that no one else is providing. Find a need and fill it. Find a hurt and heal it. Find an itch and scratch it. Virtually every successful businessperson you ask will tell you that finding and meeting unmet wants is the name of the game when it comes to winning customers. The better you do this, the more customers you'll win. The story of Jean Nidetch is a case in point.

After a lifetime of fad dieting, Jean Nidetch weighed 214 pounds. In desperation, she went to an obesity clinic and started making progress on a balanced diet. But Jean noticed something very interesting about her own behavior. It wasn't the particular diet that was causing her to lose weight as much as the emotional support of talking to others about her eating problems. So she started inviting her overweight friends over and pretty soon they were meeting every week and bringing friends with them to give and receive emotional support. That was the beginning of Weight Watchers International, Inc., a highly successful business that holds classes regularly in fifty states and twenty-six foreign countries. Today, Weight Watchers gathers additional revenues from consumer service magazines, cookbook royalties, a chain of weight-control restaurants, dietary foods, and camps for overweight children. It's a very big business and one that touches millions of customers every day.

Why did Weight Watchers become such an overwhelming success? There are a number of obvious reasons: For example, it solved a problem that plagues lots of people, and a number of people worked very hard to make it successful. But for every Jean Nidetch, there are probably hundreds of weight-loss entrepreneurs who tried and failed. The secret to Weight Watchers' initial success was that it found a hidden want and met it. While others offered diets or exercise or both, Weight Watchers offered the additional benefit of group support—and that made all the difference.

You don't have to be a genius to create customers. But you do have to find practical, workable answers to what I call the golden question:

What's the unmet want?

The art of finding and meeting the unmet want is the high road to winning customers. I call it the golden question because putting it to work is a lot like mining and selling gold. In this case, discovering an unmet want and how to satisfy it is the equivalent of prospecting for gold deposits. Some are rather obvious and easy to find while others are well hidden from view. Once you make a strike, the hard work begins. Just as with gold, you have to take the raw idea and mine it, refine it, transform it into something of value to the customer, and tell him about it. And the more you do this the richer you'll become. There is one crucial difference between unmet wants and gold. Gold is scarce but unmet wants exist in infinite quantities.

Yogi Berra said "You can observe a lot just by watching," and it's good advice for starting a search for unmet wants. Just open your eyes and look around for a problem that's bothering you, your customers, or someone you know. It may be bothering lots of other people, and if you can solve it, you're on your way. That's what Bette Nesmith did.

In 1951 Nesmith was a recently divorced, single parent working in a new job as an executive secretary at a bank. She wanted to succeed very badly but was having problems with a new innovation—the electric typewriter. Just as every solution creates new problems, the typewriter begot typos and the speed of electric typewriters increased the number of errors even more. In the hope of saving her job, Nesmith concocted a mixture of water-based paint and a coloring agent that blended with the bank's stationery. The result was a correction fluid that was so effective that other employees started asking for it, and Nesmith started bottling and selling it. By 1956, she had left the bank and was making and selling the product full time out of her garage. The business continued to grow and in 1979 the Gillette Company bought Nesmith's Liquid Paper Corporation for $47.5 million.

Bette Nesmith was smart enough to take a problem right under her nose, solve it, and capitalize on it. But if you sit around waiting for an unsolved problem to walk into your life, you may wait forever. As John H. Johnson, a leading black entrepreneur and founder of *Ebony* and *Jet* magazines, noted, "I have often said to young people, you can't go into a room, close the door, and think of a great new idea for a business. You look for a need that has to be served. You look for an opportunity to develop something . . . I never say, 'Help me because I'm black' . . . I always say, 'Let me help *you* make more money.'"

Putting the Golden Question to Work

To be sure, finding workable, profitable answers to the golden question is more an art than a science, and one that often involves a large amount of risk. You can never be sure that a new product or service is going to work. But there are some things that you can do to stack the odds more in your favor. The following ideas will help you toward that end.

1. Always start by defining markets instead of your company's talents and strengths. A classic mistake is to take the approach of, "Let's do what we do best and someone will buy it." It's the type of thinking that spawned the idea of, "Build a better mousetrap and people will beat a path to your door." But what if your customers don't have mice, or don't care about getting rid of them? Remember, value is determined by the customer's perception and not by what you or your company do well. Focus first on what customers or potential customers want or need. Then take stock of how you or your business can best meet those needs—or hire someone who can. As author and seminar leader Larry Perry puts it, "Every prosperous business or individual targets one or more needs and then takes an inventory of their unique abilities and talents. By 'meshing' talents and abilities and applying the result to satisfying one of these wants, you become prosperous—that is what we call 'nichemanship'—carving your niche in business and life."

2. *Ask your customers and potential customers the golden question.* Stay in touch with your customers and ask them what they need or want most. If you make a continuing effort to establish a good rapport with them, you'll get plenty of good ideas. (More about this in the next chapter.)

3. *Create new products and services by giving the familiar a new twist.* Studies of self-made millionaires reveal that most of them didn't make their fortunes by being an Edison, Bell, or Disney. Rather, they took an already existing product or service and made it faster, cheaper, or better, or did something to it that separated it from the rest of the competition. The Weight Watchers idea of adding group support to dieting is a case in point. Similarly, IBM, General Motors, Holiday Inns, Hilton Hotels, McDonald's, and practically every big corporation you can think of built their fortunes on products and services that existed before they did.

Coming up with a totally new product or service is extremely risky unless the need is terribly obvious. If you come up with a sure cure for baldness or cancer, or a safe oral contraceptive for males that makes the user immune to AIDS, forget the above paragraph. The world is yours for the asking. But most new products and services don't fill such obvious and urgent wants. Furthermore, when you come out with a totally new product or service you have the second job of educating potential customers about what it's for and why they should buy it. And that can be very expensive.

4. *Brainstorm ideas for creating new customers.* Write down as many answers to this question as you can think of: *What can we do that we aren't doing now to win more customers?* If you are a manager, have all of your employees answer the question. Make it a contest and give prizes and recognition to those whose ideas get put into action. And if an idea creates new customers, consider giving them a piece of the profits. This will start everyone thinking in terms of the need to create customers and give them an incentive to do so.

Millions of sales and service people talk with customers every day and get lots of great ideas about how to win new ones. But too often they are never asked for or given a reason to submit their ideas. It's a potential gold mine of information. Why not tap it?

5. *Be a trend-spotter.* The only thing we know with certainty about the future is that it's going to be different from the present. But keeping abreast of the patterns and direction of change increases the odds of your being the first to spot new opportunities. One crucial key to success in business is to ride the horse in the direction that the horse is going.

Professional trend-spotter John Naisbitt developed a rather simple way to spot trends called "content analysis." It's based on the assumption that trends start at the grass roots level and filter up to become national trends. Consequently, Naisbitt's staff reads hundreds of local newspapers each day and clips and sorts articles into categories of interest. The topics that get increasing amounts of print in local papers represent an emerging trend.

You probably don't have the time or staff to read and clip three hundred newspapers, but you can develop some useful trend-spotting skills. Write down what your customers tell you and see if you spot a recurring interest. Read and collect books and articles in your field of business and review them from time to time, looking for an emerging pattern. Attend professional meetings and make notes on what topics people are discussing. Keep abreast of broad, national trends such as those John Naisbitt identified in his book *Megatrends,* and consider their implication for your business. Making a concerted, organized effort to keep abreast of change is one of the most vital business skills you can develop. As Theodore Levitt put it, "The future belongs to people who see possibilities before they become obvious."

6. *Look before you leap.* It's easy to come up with a great new idea for a new product or service, get carried away with unabashed enthusiasm, and commit yourself to it body and soul. It's also a good way to lose your shirt. Get an objective evaluation before plowing ahead. If possible, test it on a small scale and see what happens. Get other opinions from outsiders or customers. Sleep on it. Ask yourself, "What's the worst that can happen and can I live with it?" While new products and services are important, very few are worth betting the company store on. A good rule of thumb is to earmark 15 percent of gross income for investing in new products and services. That way the business always has seed money for new projects without risking financial security.

7. *Once you decide to go ahead, move quickly.* To quote Claude McDonald, "Opportunity is a bird that never perches." While it's

important to act prudently, there's no substitute for being the first to meet an unmet want. And delaying only increases the odds of the market drying up or someone beating you to it. Once a new opportunity in the market becomes obvious, you can count on plenty of competition and a much smaller piece of the pie.

A number of Japanese companies balance prudence with action particularly well. They listen . . . and listen . . . and listen to the customer until they know precisely what he wants. Once they have a clear picture of what the customer wants, they work at breakneck speed to get the product on the market as quickly as possible.

8. Be prepared for a large number of ideas that don't work out. It's inevitable when you try new ventures that you'll have plenty of strikeouts, some base hits, and an occasional home run. But that home run will compensate for the strikeouts many times over. The key is to keep trying. IBM founder Tom Watson's formula for success was to double your number of failures. Watson reasoned that just as you can't win them all, you can't lose them all either. And as long as you keep risking, learning, and trying, success is inevitable.

8

TO KEEP CUSTOMERS FOR LIFE, ASK THE PLATINUM QUESTIONS

The only way to know how customers see your
business is to look at it through their eyes.

—DANIEL R. SCOGGIN, president and CEO, TGI Friday's, Inc.

A young boy entered a drugstore phone booth and the druggist
overheard the following conversation: "Hello, is this the Smith residence? . . . I would like to apply for the opening you have for a
gardener. . . . What's that, you already have a gardener? . . . Is he
a good gardener? . . . Are you perfectly satisfied with all of his
work? . . . Is he not doing anything that you would like to have
done? . . . Do you plan on keeping him? . . . I see. . . . Well, I'm
glad you're getting such excellent service. Thanks anyway. 'Bye."

As he left the booth the druggist remarked, "Johnny, I couldn't
help overhearing your conversation. I know it's none of my business, but aren't you the Smiths' gardener?" To which Johnny replied, "That's right. I just called to find out how I'm doing." At a
very early age, Johnny has learned that the key to keeping customers is to regularly check up on what they like and dislike about his
work.

No matter what business you're in, you can't improve on the
rewards you offer your customers until you know what they like and
dislike about the job you're doing now. And you get that precious
knowledge by asking them the platinum questions:

How are we doing?

How can we get better?

Finding the answers to those two questions tells you:

- The customer's perception of your quality of service
- What to do in order to increase that perception

Lest you forgot or missed an important point that I made earlier, let me repeat it here: *Relative quality as perceived by customers is the single most important factor in determining long-term profitability.* The big dollars aren't so much in winning as in keeping customers. And you keep them by providing greater levels of quality service as they perceive it.

The Ostrich Syndrome

Consider what happens to a business that doesn't make a regular and systematic effort to ask its customers, "How are we doing?" and, "How can we get better?" At the very least, you can be sure that it's losing a lot of repeat business and long-term big dollars. And at the very worst, this brand of ignorance is economic suicide. When it comes to winning and keeping customers, a company without a well-planned system of customer feedback is burying its head in the sand and hoping for the best. And as Dr. Robert Anthony noted, "If you stick your head in the sand, one thing is for sure, you'll get your rear kicked." Customer satisfaction is so important that you would think that most businesses would have a well-thought-out strategy for measuring it and putting this information to work.

But believe it or not, when it comes to customer satisfaction, the overwhelming majority of businesses, from giant corporations to mom and pop operations, are burying their heads in the sand and hoping for the best. Many of these same companies spare no expense to measure such things as cash flow, productivity, market share, earnings, and net assets. Yet very, very few even try to obtain, measure, or regularly monitor what the customer likes and dislikes about the job they do. It seems ironic that in the information age, most businesses aren't even trying to obtain, measure, or use some of the most valuable information of all.

In their book *A Passion for Excellence,* Tom Peters and Nancy

Austin presented some hard evidence of how most companies deal with the measurement of customer satisfaction. At a seminar with forty company presidents, all forty stated that long-term customer satisfaction was the top priority. Yet to the question, "How many of you measure any of your people on customer satisfaction?" none of the forty answered positively. A second attempt with 132 different executives attained the same results. All agreed that long-term customer satisfaction was the ultimate in performance but none were measuring it. In short, most companies don't really have a systematic measure of customer satisfaction. And of those few that do, practically none do anything of consequence with it.

Why aren't more companies measuring customer satisfaction and putting this information to work? The answer most frequently given is, "We don't know how to measure it." To be sure, customer perception is a much more fuzzy and nebulous concept to measure than cash flow, return on investment, net income, or other business indicators that can be measured in hard dollars. Yet the fact is there is no such thing as perfect information and any accountant or financial analyst will tell you that all those hard, precise numbers aren't perfect either.

Service Quality Can Be Measured

When an aging Carl Sandburg fell asleep during a young playwright's dress rehearsal, the dramatist was enraged. "How could you fall asleep," he asked, "when you know how much I wanted your opinion?" "Young man," Sandburg replied, "sleep *is* an opinion."

For better or worse your customers have an opinion about the quality of service that you offer and collecting, gathering, and measuring those opinions on a regular basis provides the crucial information that you need to keep them buying, multiplying, and coming back. Lest you think it's an impossible task, a number of companies have been doing it for some time and many more will be doing it in the future. Walker Research, Inc., of Indianapolis has been in the business of providing customer satisfaction measurements for companies for a number of years and is living testament to the fact that this type of information can be scientifically gathered and put to good use. A number of Walker's clients are using customer satisfaction measurements as one basis for determining executive bonuses.

Every satisfaction measurement program should be tailored to the specific needs of each business. For example, if you work in or own a small business with relatively few customers, regularly ask your customers the platinum questions, write down their answers and look for recurring answers suggesting strengths, weaknesses, and ideas for improvement. However, larger businesses with lots of customers may need a more organized and comprehensive approach to get an accurate reading of customer perceptions. If that's the case where you work, here are some ideas for getting the specific answers you need to the platinum questions and putting them to work.

1. Construct a brief, written survey questionnaire. You probably need more specific, targeted questions than "How are we doing?" and "How can we get better?" to get a clearer picture of what customers perceive as your strengths and weaknesses. Construct a list of questions about important, specific aspects of your service and ask the customer to rate your company from one to five or one to ten on each question. Then add a space in which the customer can tell you what he is thinking in his own words. Look, for example, at Figure 1, a comment card used by The Southland Corporation that can be found in any 7-Eleven store and mailed in postpaid by any customer. It's short, sweet, and to the point.

2. Survey your customers by telephone. Although more expensive, telephone surveys will give you the best overall picture. It takes little of the customer's time, you can ask more questions, and it provides a more random sample. Written questionnaires tend to be answered more often by customers who strongly like or dislike their experiences with your company and may not give an accurate overall picture of customer perceptions. Ask your customers specific questions about the quality of your service and ask them to rate you from one to five or one to ten on each question as you did with the written survey. Here are some questions that you may be able to use:

- How well do we deliver what we promise?
- How often do we do things right the first time?
- How often do we do things right on time?
- How quickly do we respond to your requests for service?
- How accessible are we when you need to contact us?

- How helpful and polite are we?
- How well do we speak your language?
- How well do we listen to you?
- How hard do you think we work at keeping you a satisfied customer?
- How much confidence do you have in our products or services?
- How well do we understand and try to meet your special needs and requests?
- Overall, how would you rate the appearance of our facilities, products, communications, and people?
- Overall, how would you rate the quality of our service?
- Overall, how would you rate the quality of *[your competitor's]* service?
- How willing would you be to recommend us?
- How willing would you be to buy from us again?

The more you can modify or supplement the above questions to make them applicable to your specific business, the more valuable the answers will be. For example, a telephone company may want to ask, "How accurate and timely is our billing?" Or an insurance company may want to ask, "How quickly and easily was your claim settled?" The main idea is to get an accurate reading on specific aspects of your service that the customer feels are important.

Be sure to add a few open-end questions to your list. While rating-scale questions are a basis of measurement, they may not give you valuable information that you need to hear from the customer in his own words. It usually takes a combination of well-thought-out open- and closed-end questions to give you a clear picture of perceived strengths and weaknesses. Some open-end questions you may want to ask are:

- Are we doing or not doing anything that bugs you?
- What do you like best about what we do?
- How can we better serve you?
- What parts of our service are most important to you?

Be careful with the last of these questions, because what customers say is most important may not cause them to buy. For example, airline passengers say that safety is most important, but it isn't a factor in their choice of a carrier. They assume all carriers are safe.

It isn't necessary and usually isn't possible to survey all customers. Choose a random sample of long-term customers and another sample of first-time customers to interview. That way you will get a good reading on what kinds of first impressions and lasting impressions customers are getting.

3. By all means, get feedback from your ex-customers. When customers quit, you need to know why they quit and what you can do to get them back. Send them a letter with a postpaid survey card to fill out and return. For example, the body of your letter might read:

Dear Mr. Smith:

Because your satisfaction is the key to our success, your termination of our services comes as a great disappointment. We hope that it wasn't due to a failure on our part, but if it was will you please help us by telling us where we failed you? We would greatly appreciate your taking the time to fill out the enclosed card. We strive to be the best in our field and your information is crucial to helping us improve. Thank you for your time and information and I hope we can serve you again in the near future.

Sincerely,

Like the comment card, the quit card should be short and to the point, as illustrated in Figure 2. Whatever you do, don't let regular customers quit without finding out why. If you know them personally, telephone or go see them and do whatever is reasonably possible to get them back. If you handle the situation properly, you will be able to salvage a good number of them and prevent such mishaps in the future.

4. Once you start getting information, put it to work. To put it simply, you want to capitalize on perceived strengths and correct perceived weaknesses. Get an average reading of how your team rates on each of the rating scale questions and set specific goals with deadlines for improvement in each area. Make a list of problem areas that need improvement most and rank them in order of importance. Target the most important ones for immediate improvement

OUR CONCERN IS PEOPLE.

Pleasing customers is the most important service we offer. Help us maintain the finest quality of service by answering these questions.

Check your answers on the reply card to the right. Detach the response and drop it in any mailbox.

PLEASE RATE THE FOLLOWING:

1. SPEED OF SERVICE ....
2. COURTESY OF THE EMPLOYEES ....
3. CLEANLINESS OF THE STORE ....
4. PRODUCT SELECTION — Did you find what you were looking for? ....
5. PRODUCT PRICE ....
6. PARKING LOT AND STORE EXTERIOR ......
7. How long has it been since your last visit to one of our stores? ....
8. Suggestions for additional products/services ......

Your response is sincerely appreciated.
Customer Relations 1/800-255-0711

If you wish:

Name _____
Address _____
City/State/Zip _____
Day phone # _____

	EXCELLENT	VERY GOOD	GOOD	FAIR	POOR
1.	5	4	3	2	1
2.	5	4	3	2	1
3.	5	4	3	2	1
4.	5	4	3	2	1
5.	5	4	3	2	1
6.	5	4	3	2	1

7. | 1-7 days | 8-14 days | 15-30 days | 31 + days |

8. Suggestions: _____

Date: _____ Time: _____ (a.m.) (p.m.)
Store Number/Location: _____

TEAR HERE

FIGURE 1. A CUSTOMER COMMENT CARD USED BY 7-ELEVEN STORES.

and ask everyone, "What can each of us do to improve this?" As you survey customers, be alert for problems that haven't been previously reported. Follow each one up and let the customer know what was done.

On the positive side, build on your perceived strengths as you discover them. For example, if you score high in reliability or responsiveness, your advertising and marketing can emphasize, "We deliver what we promise," or, "You know we'll be there as soon as you need us." This will remind your existing customers of the good reasons for staying with you and give potential customers a reason to buy.

5. *Keep on asking and improving.* Answers to the platinum questions will not be found with a one-shot survey; this requires a continuing process of discovering how your customers view your business over time. Survey them at least several times a year and never be satisfied with the status quo. Complacency breeds failure and self-dissatisfaction is the key to improvement. Don't blame a poor image on the economy, the weather, or your customer's intelligence. Smart organizations, like smart people, are always very tough on themselves. Everything being done today is going to be done better and differently in the future. If you don't improve, rest assured your competitor will.

Everything changes, including the customer's perception of your service. And those businesses that are smart enough to keep asking, adapting, and improving in accordance with what the customer thinks, have the inside track to long-term prosperity. It's not a guaranteed formula, but it's the way to bet.

FIGURE 2. A SURVEY CARD FORM FOR FORMER CUSTOMERS

We discontinued doing business with *(your company)* because of:

☐ The quality of merchandise

☐ The quality of service

☐ The attitude of an employee or employees

☐ Price considerations

☐ A relocation

☐ A better arrangement with a competitor

☐ A mishandled complaint

☐ Invoice or billing problems

Other reasons or comments _____

_____

_____

_____

If there was a problem, would you like one of our managers to contact you and make things right for you? _____ Yes
_____ No

Name _____

Title _____

Company _____

Address _____

City _____ State _____ Zip_____

Please fold so postage imprint shows on outside panel, tape, and return. No postage is necessary.

_____

9

THE FIVE BEST WAYS TO KEEP CUSTOMERS COMING BACK

Your customers will get better when you do.

What must a business and its employees do to establish a reputation for excellent service? Inasmuch as the customer is the final judge of service quality, the obvious thing to do is ask customers what specific aspects of service are most important to them. Extensive research has been done in this area. Some of the best research on measuring customer perceptions of service quality was done at Texas A&M University by Professors Leonard L. Berry, Valarie A. Zeithaml, and A. Parasuraman. In their research, they surveyed over nine hundred customers of diverse service businesses such as retail banking, securities brokerages, product repair and maintenance, bank credit cards, and long-distance telephone companies. What the researchers found was hardly shocking, but their findings confirm what successful customer-driven organizations have known and practiced for years. Here, in this final chapter on the basics, are the most important ingredients for providing the kind of service that keeps customers coming back. I will only touch on them briefly because we have mentioned all of these aspects previously in one form or another.

Be Reliable

Without question, *consistent performance is what customers want most*. More than anything else, the customer wants service that he can depend on. More specifically this means:

- Do what you say you are going to do
- Do it when you say you're going to do it
- Do it right the first time
- Get it done on time

One example of consistency that most of us are familiar with is McDonald's restaurants. Whenever you see the golden arches you know precisely what the food will taste like. A Big Mac is a Big Mac whether you buy it in Maine, Minneapolis, or Miami. You also know that the service will be friendly and fast, the place will be clean, and the price will be reasonable. Consistency in delivering quality food and service lies at the heart of McDonald's success.

A fanatical commitment to reliability is the key reason that Federal Express has established itself as the premier company in the overnight delivery business. They are committed to the goal of "no service failures" which means delivering all packages by 10:30 the next morning. While they may not be perfect, their track record is nothing short of astounding. For example, during one eleven-month period, Federal's Plano (North Dallas) Texas station had a success rate of 99.99 percent. In absolute numbers, the station delivered over a half a million packages with only two-hundred service failures and had no service failures for a two-month period. When you consider the number of things that can go wrong (such as traffic jams or incorrect addresses) their track record becomes even more amazing. Nevertheless, Federal Express is committed to becoming even more reliable and won't be satisfied until they have no service failures. They are smart enough to realize that even one dissatisfied customer can do a lot of damage.

On the other hand, the U.S. Post Office advertises, "We deliver excellence for less." and proudly proclaims that 97 percent of all Express Mail parcels are delivered on time the following day. In other words, they are telling you that for every half-million Express Mail packages that they deliver, thirty thousand customers are going to be disappointed (fifteen thousand senders and fifteen thousand receivers). I'm one of them. The copyedited manuscript of the book you are now reading was delivered soaking wet and a day late in a flimsy Express Mail envelope. I literally had to hang the pages out to dry before I could read them. Needless to say, the manuscript was returned to the publisher in a safe, sturdy Federal Express box.

As I mentioned at the start of the book, a typical dissatisfied customer will tell eight to ten people about his misfortune. If you multiply that by thirty thousand disappointed customers, you have between two-hundred-forty-thousand and three-hundred-thousand people hearing about a bad experience with Express Mail for every half-million packages that the U.S. Postal Service delivers. Just think about the countless thousands of people like you, who have read and will read the previous paragraph.

In business, in sports, or in any field of endeavor, consistent, high-level performance is the major difference between the champions and the also-rans. Remember, it takes twelve positive service incidents to make up for one negative incident. Your number of repeat customers will rise with the consistency of your service. Make reliability your top priority.

Be Credible

One thing customers will readily pay for is peace of mind. As customers we all willingly go back to people and businesses who sincerely want to help us and have our best interests at heart. We want security, integrity, and the assurance that if there is a problem, it will be promptly handled at no extra cost. We don't want hidden agendas, hard sell techniques, extra charges, and contracts with "fine print." If we buy products, we want them to be safe and guaranteed. If we buy services, such as medical, legal, or financial services, we want them to be free from danger, risk, or doubt and kept confidential. Such is the nature of credibility.

I purchased the personal computer that I am now using from a local department store because of the helpfulness of the salesperson and the store's reputation for "no risk" shopping. Sure, I could have purchased it out of town cheaper and saved paying sales tax. But I was a computer novice and Tony (the salesperson) installed the computer on my desk and showed me how to use it. After I had been using the machine for about three weeks, the screen suddenly went blank. I called the store and the next day Tony picked up the computer and gave me a brand new one that has worked well for the past two years. Credibility brings customers back.

Be Attractive

Appearances can be deceiving, but customers draw a lot of conclusions about the quality of service on the basis of what they see. As one airline chairman put it, "Coffee stains on the flip-down trays mean (to the customer) that we do our engine maintenance wrong." Anything the customer sees, feels, touches, hears, or smells concerning your business is shaping his opinion of your service for better or worse. Reread recommendation 2 in Chapter 6 (p. 54), about looking at your business through your customer's eyes, and make the effort to put forth a first-class image. It's not a frivolous expense. It's an investment.

Be Responsive

In a hotel grill in Hungary, each table is equipped with a ten-minute hourglass. If your order isn't taken in ten minutes, the meal is free. Like it or not, we live in an era of instant everything. When customers want service, they want it now.

Being responsive means being accessible, available, and willing to help customers whenever they have a problem. It also means keeping them informed and providing the service as soon as possible. For example, one evening my kitchen sink stopped up and I called a local plumbing service. The service assured me that a plumber would be out that evening. Ten minutes later, the service called back and told me that a plumber would be there within the next hour. Thirty minutes later the plumber appeared and unstopped the sink, I paid him, and the problem was solved. An hour later the service called to make sure everything was okay. Several days later I received a letter thanking me for my patronage, and enclosed was a decal with the name and telephone number of the service. I promptly placed the decal on the garbage disposal under the kitchen sink. Whenever I have a plumbing problem, guess who I call?

Be Empathic

Every customer is a special individual who wants to be treated as such. He has his own unique personality, wants, and reasons for buying. And to the extent that you treat him as someone special and solve his unique problems, he will continue to be your customer.

Being empathic means putting yourself in the customer's shoes, trying to grasp his point of view and feeling what he feels. It means listening intently, asking the right questions, speaking his language, and tailoring your services to help him as best you can. Don't treat him the way you want to be treated. He's a different person with different problems and a different point of view. Instead, treat him the way he wants to be treated. Customers buy for their reasons and not ours. Fred Aubert, the clothing salesperson you read about in Chapter 2, is an excellent example of winning and keeping customers with empathy.

So there you have the five major factors on which customers judge the quality of service: reliability, credibility, appearance, responsiveness, and empathy. Commit them to memory by remembering the words, "reliable care." The word "reliable" will remind you that reliability is what customers value most, and the word "care" is an acronym for the other four factors: C for credibility, A for appearance, R for responsiveness and E for empathy. Taking reliable care of your customers is what keeps them buying, multiplying, and coming back.

Part Two

MANAGING THE MOMENTS OF TRUTH:
Ten Action-Ready Strategies

INTRODUCTION

Everyone is trying to accomplish something big,
not realizing that life is made up of little things.

—FRANK A. CLARK

You now have a good, overall understanding of what it takes to win and keep customers. The next step is to put those ideas to work at the moments of truth—those moments of customer contact. Whenever you or anyone else who works for your company has contact with a customer, be it in person, by telephone, or through the mail, the customer will come away feeling better, worse, or the same about your company. If the customer's experience is rewarding, chances are he will buy, recommend you to others, and come back. If his experience is neutral, he may or may not come back. But if he walks away feeling negative, he probably won't be back and will likely tell up to twenty other people. In short, your job is to reward each customer at the moment of truth to make him feel positive about you and your company.

Jan Carlzon, president of Scandinavian Airlines Systems, believes that the key to a profitable service business is how well the moments of truth are managed. Carlzon realized that SAS flew 10 million passengers per year and that each passenger came in contact with an average of five SAS employees, for a total of 50 million moments of truth each year. Managing the moments of truth became a top priority at SAS. All employees went through an intense training program, with plenty of follow-up to reinforce the message. And with that basic strategy SAS was transformed from an 8-million-dollar money loser to a 71-million-dollar money maker in less than one year.

Excellent service isn't the result of doing any one thing 1,000 percent better. It's the result of doing thousands of things 1 percent better. Each of the following ten chapters explains how to reward the customer at a given moment of truth to make his experience a positive one. Inasmuch as every business is unique, there is no way I can cover every possible moment of truth. Consequently, I have chosen ten moments of truth that are common to customer contact situations in almost every business. These ten action-ready strategies will help to turn people into customers and customers into lifetime partners.

10

What to Do When the Customer

APPEARS, CALLS, OR INQUIRES

You never get a second chance to make a good first impression.

—ANONYMOUS

Mark Sanborn is an author and professional speaker whom I have had the pleasure of knowing for the past several years. In November 1984 he went shopping for a personal computer. I'll let him tell you what happened:

I decided to purchase a personal computer last November to gain the benefit of word processing as well as some tax benefits. I told every salesman I talked with my hardware and software needs, how much I was willing to spend and that I intended to purchase by December 31. A salesman at the top rated computer store in the city rattled off estimates but couldn't be bothered to write down any package prices so I could compare elsewhere. When I asked for a card, he replied, "I don't normally work at this store so you probably wouldn't find me here later anyhow." I made an appointment when I visited the next store. Within 5 minutes of arriving, the owner instructed me to "play around with some of the machines" while he assisted someone who had just wandered in.

I was encouraged by the amount of time the third salesman I talked with devoted to me. He suggested a package and price that I was happy with. The monitor I wanted to see before buying was to arrive in the next 10 days. He promised to call me when it came in to finalize the deal. He never did.

The moral of the story: This newsletter is being written on my old Smith-Corona, not a PC.*

Mark knew what he wanted, was prepared to buy it, and wanted someone to help him make an intelligent choice and appreciate his business. Yet in three separate incidents he was treated more like an inconvenience than an asset. As customers you and I know that this type of treatment is all too common.

Humorist Robert Henry, another outstanding professional speaker, had a similar but much stranger experience. One evening about six, Robert walked into a discount department store in Columbus, Georgia, to buy a pair of binoculars. As he walked up to the appropriate counter he noticed that he was the only customer in the store. Behind the counter were two salespersons. One was so preoccupied talking to "Mama" on the telephone that she refused to acknowledge that Robert was there. At the other end of the counter, a second salesperson was unloading inventory from a box onto the shelves. Growing impatient, Robert walked down to her end of the counter and just stood there. Finally, she looked up at Robert and said, "You got a number?"

"I got a what?" asked Robert, trying to control his astonishment at such an absurdity.

"You got a number? You gotta have a number."

Robert replied, "Lady, I'm the only customer in the store! I don't need a number. Can't you see how ridiculous this is?" But she failed to see the absurdity and insisted that Robert take a number before agreeing to wait on him. By now, it was obvious to Robert that she was more interested in following procedures than helping the customer. So, he went to the take-a-number machine, pulled number 37 and walked back to the salesperson. With that, she promptly went to her number counter, which revealed that the last customer waited on had been holding number 34. So she screamed out, "35! . . . 35! . . . 36! . . . 36! . . . 37!"

---

*Mark Sanborn, *Great Ideas* (Mark Sanborn Associates, 249 Pine Street, First Floor, Philadelphia, PA 19106, January–February 1985), pp. 1–2.

"I'm number 37," said Robert.

"May I help you?" she asked, without cracking a smile.

"No," replied Robert, and he turned around and walked out.

The most crucial contact of all is the first one that the customer makes with your business, because if you lose him here, he's likely lost forever. This makes it imperative that those having initial contact with customers do their utmost to help the customer and make him feel appreciated, rather than treating him like an interruption. L. L. Bean in Freeport, Maine, prominently displays a poster around its headquarters that expresses the idea best:

WHAT IS A CUSTOMER?

A Customer is the most important
person ever in this office . . . in person or by mail.

A Customer is not dependent on us . . .
we are dependent on him.

A Customer is not an interruption of
our work . . . he is the purpose of it. We are
not doing a favor by serving him . . . he is doing us a
favor by giving us the opportunity to do so.

A Customer is not someone to argue or match
wits with. Nobody ever won an argument with a customer.

A Customer is a person who brings us his wants. It is
our job to handle them profitably to him and ourselves.

Promptness and Preparation Are the Keys

Rewarding a customer at the initial moment of truth begins long before he ever appears, writes, calls, or agrees to see you. It takes a sound, well-thought-out strategy and a good deal of groundwork to make first contacts successful. Putting the following ideas to work will help you and those you work with make a positive first impression.

1. As soon as you see a customer, politely acknowledge his presence. Never, never, never, ever ignore a customer. There is absolutely no excuse for it. I don't care if you have ten customers ahead of him and three on hold on the telephone. Almost everyone will be understanding of your predicament and most will be willing to wait if you make the effort to say something like, "Thank you for coming in. I'll be with you as soon as I can." It's when the customer feels that you don't know or don't care that he is there that you're most likely to lose him.

2. Be equally prompt and polite when answering the telephone. Letting the telephone ring forever before answering it and answering with "Ajax Widgets, please hold" are real turn-offs that make customers feel ignored. If you get lots of calls and can't handle them, consider hiring a secretary or an answering service to take your calls, or buy a telephone answering machine.

If a customer telephones while you are occupied, politely tell him you're tied up and ask if you may call him back. If he opts for the call back, specify a mutually agreeable time and stick to it. If you can help him in less than one minute, ask if he would like to hold or if he would prefer that you call him back. If he holds, be sure to thank him for holding. Give each customer on the telephone your undivided attention and best positive attitude. Monotone, routine answers, shuffling papers, or answering questions from others tell the customer that you don't think his call is all that important.

3. If a customer has a scheduled appointment, make it your business to be on time. If you can't be on time, telephone and tell him how much you are behind schedule and ask if the delay is acceptable or if he would prefer to reschedule. (I sure hope some doctors read this.) Respecting the customer's time is a common courtesy that all are entitled to. My dentist, Debra Arnold, does this, and that's one reason I am her loyal patient.

Needless to say, mail inquiries should be followed up with all due speed as well. Whenever a customer writes, calls, appears, or agrees to see you the first thing he wants is prompt attention. Reward him with it.

4. Prepare for customers' questions by having the answers before they ask. There are few things more impressive than an employee equipped with the knowledge and ability to help customers solve their problems. Conversely, an employee without the knowledge or willingness to help almost guarantees a lost customer. Evangelist Billy Graham tells of the time he arrived in a small town to preach a sermon. He wanted to mail a letter and asked a young boy how to get to the post office. The young boy told him and Graham said, "Thank you. If you'll come to the Baptist church this evening, you can hear me telling everyone how to get to Heaven."

"I don't think I'll be there," replied the boy. "You don't even know your way to the post office."

Like the young boy, customers evaluate the competence of a business largely on the basis of how much employees appear to know. Develop a list of things to find out about every product or service you work with. You may want to start with such basic questions as these:

- What is it?
- What does it do?
- What are the major benefits to the customer? (What good feelings or solutions to problems does it provide?)
- What does it cost?
- Why is it worth more than it costs?
- What's the competition and why is ours a better value?

Write down questions that customers frequently ask you and make sure you have thorough answers to them. If a customer asks a question that you cannot answer, be honest and tell him, "I don't know but I can find out and I'll give you the answer tomorrow" (or better yet, today). Then find out and make good on your promise. Most initial moments of truth involve questions that the customer has. Your job is to be able to answer them on the spot.

5. *Whenever possible, prepare in advance for each individual customer.* When Douglas MacArthur was supreme commander in charge of Japan after World War II, he would have an aide write a report of every visiting dignitary's background and interests. Equipped with this knowledge, he was able to converse with each visitor on an informed level about what interested the visitor most. Visitors left feeling amazed and terribly flattered. As a result, MacArthur made a lot of friends and sold a lot of people on his policies.

The more you know about each individiual customer, the easier it is to serve him and establish a lasting relationship. Chances are you don't have the resources of Douglas MacArthur and writing a report on each customer is probably out of the question. But you can read up on a customer's specific company or industry before calling to get an idea of how you can serve that customer. And you can prepare a list of questions to ask when you meet. If you are a salesperson, odds are that you spend only about one-fourth of your workday in actual selling. Spend the other three-fourths preparing for your customers. Use the time to set specific goals. Briefly write down in a sentence or two what you want to accomplish before seeing each customer. Carry reading material or cassette tapes that will make you a better prepared and informed professional. Obviously, if you deal with hundreds of customers every day, you can't do this. But if you're a salesperson trying to make an important sale, it's clearly in your best interest to know as much about each customer as you can and decide what you want to achieve. The will to win is meaningless without the will to prepare.

6. *Start each day with a checkup.* As mentioned earlier, first impressions will be based largely on your appearance and those of your materials and place of business, and on anything the customer sees, feels, smells, hears, or tastes. Make a list of things that need to be checked at the start of each day to make sure the customer gets a good first impression. Start with yourself. Are you clear-eyed, well groomed, well dressed, and free of bad breath or body odors? Are your business cards and sales materials clean and crisp? Is the place clean and orderly? In short, are you and your colleagues physically and mentally prepared to give every customer a first-class performance? Take a little extra time at the start of each day to look at the business through your customer's eyes. That way you'll be giving yourself every possible chance to make this initial moment of truth a rewarding one for both you and your customers.

7. *Ask the right questions.* You can't help the customer if you don't know what his wants, needs, and problems are. And the best way to find out is to simply ask him. Begin with broad, open-ended, nonthreatening questions and encourage him to do the talking. When he says something you want to hear more about, nod your head (a subtle reward) and say, "Can you tell me more about that?" If you have to ask a tension-raising question like, "How much do you want to spend?" explain that you need to know this to deter-

mine if you can help him. Some examples of good open-ended questions are:

- What are you trying to accomplish?
- What do you know about our products and services?
- How would you like me to work with you?
- How soon do you need this?
- How can we be of greatest help to you?

No matter what questions you ask, they should reflect the attitude of a concerned, sincere, helpful person.

8. Listen for total meaning. All too often, we don't really hear what the other person is telling us. Instead, we concentrate on what we are going to say and miss a lot of the message.

Being a good listener means much more than simply hearing what people are saying. It means blocking out all distractions, giving the customer your undivided attention, and listening with your whole self. A wise man once remarked that we should learn to listen with three ears:

- Listen to what people are saying
- Listen for what they are not saying
- Listen for what people would like to say but can't put into words

For example, a real-estate agent credits much of his success to paying attention to what the client says and how he says it. "Nothing is too good for my family," says one client. But he says it with a hesitant voice and a tight smile and the agent senses a conflict between what the client wants and what he can afford. When that happens the agent says, "Maybe you'd like to look at a few more houses," and suggests some in a lower price range. Because of total listening, the agent gets a satisfied customer and referrals that will lead to future sales, and the client gets a home he can afford.

Never underestimate the value of listening to the customer. It's one of the most valuable skills you can learn.

9. Match your solutions with their problems. Once you have identified what they want or need, you can intelligently explain how you can help them and offer to do so. If you don't feel you can really help them, be honest and say so. Recommend someone who can help and ask to be of service in the future.

10. Make them feel good about being your customer. Always thank them for the opportunity to help and reassure them that they make a wise choice when they buy from you. Then back up those words with good actions. Remember, rewarding the customer is the name of the game.

What to Do When the Customer
11
IS ANGRY OR DEFENSIVE

My life is in the hands of any fool who makes me
lose my temper.

—JOSEPH HUNTER

"Take your damn policy and shove it! That's the most stupid thing
I've ever heard."

"What do you mean you can't cash this check? I've been shopping
here for twenty years."

"I don't give a #%* about your @%& regulations! Just get this
damned airplane off the ground and get me home!"

If you work with customers, you know that not all of them behave
like angels. Customers are people and from time to time we all have
a tendency to act like the north end of a southbound horse—espe-
cially when we are angry or upset. How do you handle an irate
customer and keep him? We will get to the specifics shortly, but let's
begin answering that question by profiting from the experiences of
Bob and Al.

When Bob and Al finished college, they both took jobs handling
complaints and returns at a large department store. Needless to say,
their academic training hardly prepared them for what they experi-
enced. Every day they faced a seemingly endless stream of angry,
defensive, belligerent customers who all had problems and wanted
them solved, *"right now!"* If it wasn't the wrong merchandise, it was
the wrong size. And if it was the right merchandise and the right

size, it didn't work properly. It seemed to Bob and Al that every customer was, in effect, telling them, "I've got a problem and it's all your fault."

It didn't take long for this kind of treatment to take its toll. Bob and Al went home each night feeling exhausted and irritable. In an attempt to cope, they tried a number of strategies at work. First, they tried fighting back, but that only made matters worse. Then they tried reacting to customers with a cool, detached indifference, but that didn't work either. Finally, they just tried being quietly patient, but they still went home feeling burned out. Relationships with friends and families began to suffer and they were on the verge of looking for other work.

One evening after work, they stopped off at a bar and started talking about the job and how it was getting to them. They agreed that the heart of the problem was that they were letting negative customer attitudes put them on the defensive. They were so conditioned to expect trouble that whenever a customer appeared, they were always tense and anticipating trouble—and the customers sensed it.

Just as they were about to agree that quitting was the only option left, they spotted a sign tacked up behind the bar that read: *Be kind. Everyone you meet is fighting a tough battle.*

That was when they realized that kindness was the one thing that they had not tried. The next day, instead of waiting for customers to attack, they took the initiative and set the tone by reaching out with understanding and friendship. Each customer was greeted with a friendly smile, courteous service, and a pledge to do whatever they could to help solve their problems as quickly as possible. At the end of the day they felt much better and over the next few days they worked on perfecting their technique. Pretty soon, they were changing frowns into smiles and some customers actually began laughing and joking with them.

A few weeks later, Bob remarked to Al, "You know what? Something has happened in this place. We're starting to get a better class of people."

You don't have to work in a complaint department to catch a lot of flack from irate customers. If you work in a service job, it comes with the territory. What the customer is upset about usually isn't your fault. But he doesn't care about that. He's just mad, and to him, you're the company that's causing all of his misery.

You Can React Defensively or Helpfully

Whenever you encounter an angry or defensive customer you have a choice. You can react either defensively or helpfully. Bob and Al first reacted defensively. They didn't know any better, and when angry customers confronted them, they either responded in kind, reacted indifferently, or gave customers the silent treatment. And as they found out, being on the defensive doesn't help the customer to feel one bit better, doesn't solve the problem, and is an exhausting way to live.

Reacting to angry people with a defensive attitude is only asking for more abuse. You might as well hang a "kick me" sign around your neck. We teach others how to treat us with our own behavior. And if you are contiually being mistreated, chances are you're cooperating with the treatment.

Reward with Kindness, Empathy, and Solutions

The problem of an irate customer is actually two problems in one. First, you have to deal with the customer's feelings. Then you have to try as best you can to solve the problem that made him mad in the first place. If you simply solve the problem without making an effort to soothe his anger, he probably won't be back. Remember, people come back to buy where they feel good. The next time you encounter an angry customer, keep these ideas in mind and put them to work.

1. Keep your cool. If you are right there's no reason to lose your temper. If you're wrong, you can't afford to lose it. Never allow the customer to put you on the defensive. It's only normal to want to defend yourself when a customer verbally assaults you, but it only makes things worse. Lashing back or saying, "Don't blame me. I didn't do it," or making excuses will only make him angrier. As Abigail Van Buren noted, "People who fight fire with fire usually end up with ashes."

One of the worst things you can do is argue with the customer. If you make him look foolish, he will find a way to fight back and you'll lose a customer. If you allow him to make you look foolish, he will think you're dumb, and nobody wants to buy from dumb people. Going on the defensive is a lose-lose situation.

Instead, take the offensive with a positive approach. Get on the same physical level as the other person. Keep a comfortable distance and look him in the eyes with the expression of someone who is concerned about his problem. Respond to his comments with something like, "I'm sorry you're upset. Let's see what we can do to solve this problem and make things right for you."

Keep in mind that the angry customer is the one with the problem. It's him and not you who has lost his cool. Let him blow off steam and calm down. If his tirade is distracting or obnoxious to others, invite him to a more private place to hear him out. And don't take his remarks personally. Angry people say all sorts of irrational things that they don't mean. When a customer is critical he is also giving you information. Concentrate on listening for information that will help you solve the problem, rather than taking the criticism personally.

2. Listen with empathy and for the facts. An angry customer will usually respond well if he feels that you really care about his problem and are trying to feel what he is feeling. Treating his problem as if it's routine or asking him to fill out a form without first listening to him is just asking for more trouble. Angry people demand to be heard and understood.

As you listen, look for areas of agreement and agree with the customer whenever you can. Statements such as, "I understand why you're angry," "I agree that this is quite an inconvenience for you," and, "If I were you I would be mad too," will show the customer you are empathizing and trying to understand him.

Most customers will start to calm down after you listen to their initial outbursts. Your next step is to become a problem-solver while continuing to be a hand-holder. If you haven't already identified the problem or the cause of the problem, start asking the customer questions that give you this information, such as, "What went wrong?" "What did you do then?" "Who told you that?" "Can you tell me more about that?" If appropriate, take notes. Nod your head in agreement when you want the customer to keep talking. Paraphrase important points and ask him, "Do I have that correct?"

3. Take action to solve the customer's problem. Once you have a good grasp of the problem, do what you can to help the customer as much as you can. If possible, offer the customer several options and let him choose. If you can't solve the problem for him, refer him to someone who can and do what you can to put him in contact with the problem-solver. And if your company is at fault, by all means, apologize profusely.

One important point must be stressed. When you offer the customer solutions to his dilemma, state them positively. Tell him what you can do rather than what you cannot do. For example, don't say, "We aren't open on Sundays." Instead say, "We are open until 1:00 P.M. Saturday to serve you." Don't say, "I can't get you a refund today." Say, "I'll have your refund check first thing in the morning."

4. Bring the incident to a polite close. Once you have solved the customer's problem or done what you can to resolve it, ask him, "Is there any other way I can be of help to you today?" Assuming the answer is no, thank the customer for telling you his concern. While you may find it strange to thank someone who just gave you a hard time, keep in mind that he may have provided you with information that will prevent this problem in the future and keep you from losing customers. A customer with the passion to get angry also has the ability to be loyal. Remember, it's the nice customers who quietly walk away and don't come back that do the most damage.

When appropriate, make a follow-up call to the customer to make sure that the problem was properly solved or that a resolution is underway. This all-important finishing touch tells the customer that his problems are your utmost concern. As one upset customer remarked, "I was angry at the time and I thought I would never go back. However, the manager called me a couple of weeks later and seemed really concerned that I had not been coming in. I knew then that he really cared." As always, thank the customer for the opportunity to be of service.

5. Don't expect to win them all. No matter how patient, helpful, and understanding you are, there will be a small percentage of irate customers that it's impossible to satisfy. Unfortunately, some customers are just plain angry, and get their satisfaction from giving others a hard time. If you have someone who refuses to calm down or insists on being obnoxious despite your best efforts, calmly tell him, "If we are going to continue to do business it has to be a good deal for both of us." Then calmly offer him a refund, if he is entitled to one, and move on. If a customer shows definite signs of becoming hostile or violent, don't try to handle it alone. Get help from higher management or the authorities.

Dealing with angry, upset customers takes a wealth of self-control and is a tough job for the best of us. If you deal with them regularly, find an emotional outlet for the tension that you're bound to build up inside. Play tennis, swim, walk, beat a pillow, jog, or get a punching bag. And don't expect to always be perfect in dealing with angry customers. You're human too. As Elliott Hubbard put it, "Every man is a damn fool for at least five minutes out of every day. Wisdom consists of not exceeding the limit."

What to Do When the Customer

12

HAS SPECIAL REQUESTS

Barber: How would you like your hair cut, sir?
George S. Kaufman: In perfect silence.

In the 1970 film *Five Easy Pieces*, Jack Nicholson goes into a road-side café and asks for an order of eggs and a side order of wheat toast. The waitress tells him that wheat toast isn't on the menu and the rules forbid her to serve substitutes. Looking over the menu, Nicholson notices that they serve a chicken salad sandwich on whole wheat. He tries several times to talk the waitress into bringing him an order of wheat toast, but she just gets irritated and points to a sign that reads, NO SUBSTITUTES and WE RESERVE THE RIGHT TO REFUSE SERVICE TO ANYONE. Finally, Nicholson orders a chicken salad sandwich on wheat toast, hold the mayonnaise, hold the but-ter, hold the lettuce. As the waitress repeats the order, Nicholson angrily adds, "Now all you have to do is hold the chicken salad, bring me the damn whole wheat toast, give me a check for the chicken salad sandwich, and you haven't broken any rules." Un-wisely, the waitress asks where she should hold the chicken salad. Nicholson snidely replies, "Between your knees," and walks out. A dissatisfied customer.

If you saw *Five Easy Pieces*, you probably remember that scene better than any other in the entire film because you can readily identify with it. It's all too common to go to a business with special requests and have them rebuffed or ignored. It's the kind of treatment that turns nice customers into ex-customers and profits into losses. Many years ago when General Motors started producing cars with various styles, options, and colors, Henry Ford insisted on mass producing only one standardized model and remarked, "The customer can have a car in any color as long as it's black." At one time, Ford held two-thirds of the automobile market, and there is little doubt that Ford's refusal to accommodate different customer tastes and preferences opened the door for General Motors to capture the leading share of the United States automobile market. While that history lesson goes back many years, its message is forever valuable:

Customize: Give each customer exactly what he wants.

Every customer is an individual person or group of people having special wants and needs. And the better you meet those unique wants and needs, the greater are the odds of winning and keeping those customers. The case of Don, an industrial supply sales rep, is a case in point.

Don received a call early one day from a new customer who was having problems with one of his machines. Don hadn't sold him the machine, but the customer valued Don's mechanical expertise and asked if he would mind coming by to look at it. When he arrived, Don listened to the machine and initially diagnosed the problem as faulty bearings. Don then proceeded to roll up his sleeves, take the machine apart, and inspect the bearings. Needless to say, Don's hands became covered with oil and grease, but he didn't mind and remarked "Dirt washes off" to the concerned customer.

It turned out that faulty bearings were the problem. Don's company didn't carry the particular type, so he gave the customer the name and address of a competitor who carried them. The customer thanked Don for all his help and Don left.

But when Don returned to his office that afternoon, he found that the customer had ordered the replacement bearings from Don's company. He knew that Don would have to buy the bearings from the competitor and resell them to him, but he wanted Don to get credit and commission for the sale. It was his way of saying, "Thanks for going the extra mile." And since that day he has been Don's loyal customer.

Five Excellent Reasons for Customizing

You may be thinking, "Customizing takes a whole lot of extra time and effort and I'm not sure that it's worth it where I work." Well, more often than not, the extra time and effort invested has a handsome payoff. Here's why:

1. It shows people that you really care about serving them. Customers will listen to what you say but they will believe what you do. The better you tailor your products and services to their individual needs, the more readily they will perceive you as someone offering products or services of genuine value to them.

2. It gives you and your team a source of pride and confidence. When you make the effort to learn and react to each customer's unique needs, you have the pride and confidence of knowing that you can help each customer and give him real value for his dollars.

3. It's great for repeat business. Look at your own behavior as a customer. Would you rather buy from someone who treats you like a number, or from someone who takes the time to treat you like a special person and find out your unique wants? Time and again it's been shown that people come back to buy where they get special treatment.

4. It overcomes customer defensiveness and gains you quicker acceptance. If you work as a sales rep, it's common to have prospective customers tell you something like, "OK, let's hear your story. Give me the pitch." But by taking a customizing approach, you can reply with something like, "My story doesn't matter as much as yours does. Let's decide if and how I might be able to help you." Customizing is helping people to buy what's best for them, and as I pointed out in Chapter 2, it's hard to resist someone who sincerely wants to help.

5. It virtually eliminates the competition. Author and consultant Phil Wexler refers to this strategy as putting the golden handcuffs on the client. When you know more about the customer than your competition does, and meet his needs better than your competition does, you (in effect) have no competition. Your customers will come to rely on you and may even consider you a part of their business or their lives. Because you take such special care of them you can tell them, "You get me with every purchase." And that's the one thing that no one else can offer.

The Mark of Professionalism

In today's world, professionalism has little to do with what you do for a living. It's how well you do what you do that separates the pros from the also-rans. The mark of a true professional is that by his conduct he gives the customer excellent value for his dollars as the customer perceives it. And there is no better way to build perceived value than by tailoring your efforts to benefit each individual customer. Keep these ideas in mind as you strive to reward with customization.

1. Fill any and all special requests as best you can. At TGI Friday's, Inc., all employees are schooled in the *Five Easy Pieces* theory of service. Simply put, this theory means that good service requires going beyond the ordinary and doing whatever is reasonable to give the customer what he wants. A Friday's customer can order whatever he wants, even if the item isn't on the menu. If all the ingredients are in the kitchen (and they normally are), the customer's request will be filled.

You don't have to be in the restaurant business to put the *Five Easy Pieces* theory to work. But you do have to be thoughtful, accommodating, and flexible toward your customers and the products and services you offer. Make an extra effort to reward those special requests. It will pay you back many times over.

2. Search for unmet wants in each customer and meet them. Ask your customers the golden and platinum questions. What do they need that's not being provided? How can you serve them better? What do they like most about your products and services? What do they like least? If you have contact with regular customers, keep records on each one and write down any comments that are revealing or interesting. If you promise to do a favor for them, write it down and follow through. (Confucius say poor handwriting better than good memory.) Your customers can't help but be impressed by your making that extra effort to remember their special wants and needs and helping them.

3. Treat each person and his requests as unique and special. I know that I'm repeating myself, so I won't belabor the point. When people have a special request, see to it that they walk away from that moment of truth feeling that you cared about them and did the best you could to help.

Some years ago, a young couple walked into a small jewelry store and asked the clerk if he could make the boy's class ring fit the girl's finger. The clerk installed a $1.50 ring guard while they waited. While the clerk was installing the ring guard, the couple remarked that the people at the big jewelry store around the corner had been too busy to help them.

Later that year, the same couple came back and bought over a thousand dollars' worth of jewelry. And two years later, the little jewelry store moved around the corner. The big one had gone out of business.

Don't homogenize. Customize!

13 What to Do When the Customer
CAN'T MAKE UP HIS MIND

They [customers] want someone to come in and
say "Dammit, this is what you should do. Now."

—ROBERT LONDON, director of sales, Montgomery Securities

At one time or another, all of us want to buy something but don't know how to go about making an intelligent choice. Here are several personal experiences that come to mind.

Case 1. I was speaking in Singapore a few years ago and went shopping for a camera, not knowing the first thing about them. When I confessed my ignorance to the salesperson, he immediately recommended a particular automatic camera. It takes great pictures, is easy to use, and is virtually idiot-proof—just what I needed. I took his recommendation and have enjoyed the camera thoroughly.

Case 2. I wanted to buy a personal computer for word processing and business applications. After listening to me, the salesperson recommended an Apple Macintosh and told me why, and I bought one. I have been happy with it ever since.

Case 3. Fred Siegel, an investment counselor, knows a whole lot more about the stock market and investments than I do. Consequently, I let him choose the investments for my portfolio, and he does a fine job.

In all three of the above cases, I am a satisfied customer because the salesperson is helping me solve my problems by recommending an intelligent choice. In effect, I am telling them, "You know a whole lot more about what you sell than I do. Recommend something for me, tell me why, and if it sounds good, I'll buy it." They recommended and I bought.

Consider what would have happened if the camera salesperson had responded with, "All of our cameras are good. Just pick out one in your price range." Do you really think I would have bought a camera from him? What if the computer rep had said, "I don't really know enough about you to make an intelligent recommendation. Why don't you take these brochures home and decide which one you like best." Do you think I would have come back with an order? What if Fred had said, "Call me after you read the stock page and tell me what you want to buy and sell." Would I still be investing with Fred? Not on your life.

One major obstacle that frequently prevents customers from buying is the stress of making a decision. An indecisive customer is afraid of making a bad choice and getting stuck with the consequences. And the greater the purchase, the greater the fear. As a result, it's common for customers to get caught up in the paralysis-by-analysis syndrome. They get so involved in agonizing over what to buy that they never get around to buying. Whenever you have an indecisive customer:

Reward Indecision with Recommendations

More often than not, an indecisive customer wants you to take the weight of decision-making off his shoulders, recommend a choice for him, and reassure him that he is doing the right thing. Do it. The message you want to convey, in a sincere, confident manner, is, "Buy this. It will solve your problems." Then explain why your recommendation is a good one. More specifically, here are some guidelines to follow the next time you encounter a customer who cannot make up his mind:

1. Make sure that the customer has the authority to make a buying decision. As sales trainer and consultant Alan Cimberg puts it, "If you're selling hand organs, make sure you aren't speaking to the monkey." Very often a customer knows what he or she wants but the final decision is going to be made by the boss, the spouse, a committee, or someone else. If you suspect that this may be the case, ask if someone else will be involved in making the purchasing decision. People without the authority to make a decision usually won't tell you, unless you ask. There's a big difference between those who are reluctant to make a decision and those who can't. All the reasons and recommendations in the world are useless until you put them in front of the decision maker.

2. *Ask, listen, and learn before recommending.* In medicine, prescription without diagnosis is malpractice. Take a similar approach with your customers and find out what their problems, needs, tastes, and preferences are before offering a recommendation. Questions that begin with "who," "what," "where," "when," "why," and "how" are usually the best for finding out what a customer's wants and needs are. For example, if you are a travel agent and a customer comes in trying to decide where to take his next vacation, you might ask such questions as:

- Who else, if anyone, will be going with you?
- What kind of weather or climate do you prefer for a vacation?
- What's your idea of a great vacation?
- When do you plan on going?
- Where have you been on vacation before?
- How much are you budgeting for your vacation?
- How much time do you have?

Make up your own list of questions that you can ask customers when they inquire about your products or services. With practice, you'll learn which questions are best at pinpointing the customer's wants and discover new and better questions to ask. Keep updating, refining, and improving your list. You'll make more sales, help more customers, and save a lot of time and energy when you're armed with the right questions.

3. *Make a recommendation and tell the customer why.* As pointed out earlier, people buy emotionally and justify with logic. In most cases the undecided buyer wants you to make the buying decision for him and give him one or two reasons to convince him that it's the right choice. If the reasons make sense to him, chances are that he will buy. For example, when I went camera shopping, the salesperson recommended the automatic camera and then convinced me that it was practically impossible to take a bad picture with it, de-

spite my inexperience. When I went computer shopping, the computer sales rep recommended the Macintosh because it was the easiest machine to master word processing on. "You'll be doing word processing on it in an hour or two," he promised. In both cases, the reasons sounded good to me, and I bought. Most important, the reasons that they gave turned out to be true and not empty promises. Based on what you learn about each customer, give him one or more reasons why your particular recommendation will be most beneficial to him.

4. Don't give the customer too many options. Even if you know that there are lots of choices, just pick one or two, recommend them and tell why. Too many choices is a major cause of indecision and can only frustrate an already indecisive customer.

Another personal example comes to mind. Some time back I went to an eye doctor to try to solve the problem of blurred vision in one eye. After an examination, the doctor determined that increased astigmatism was causing the problem. But instead of recommending a course of action, he gave me a lengthy monologue on all the options that were available. He could give me a stronger power contact lens that would improve my distance vision, but I would have to wear glasses for reading. Or he could give me a special astigmatic lens that costs three times more and might not be as comfortable as what I now have. Or he could fit me in gas permeable hard lenses. Or we could do nothing, because my vision wasn't that bad to begin with. He gave me lots of options but wouldn't recommend one.

I left his office feeling frustrated. I went to him with a problem and I wanted a solution. I didn't want a discourse on the state of the art of contact lenses. I wanted to see better. Although I couldn't express it at the time, a little voice inside me was saying, "Dammit, you're the doctor. You know much, much more about eye care than I ever will. Make a decision. If you lead, I'll follow." Yet the man in charge wouldn't take charge. A friend of mine had a similar experience with the same doctor, and both of us have since taken our eye care needs elsewhere.

5. Be caring, confident, and decisive in your tone of voice and behavior. Indecisive buyers will respond to firmness and decisive action because that's precisely what they are looking for. Some years ago, Jim, an office supplies salesman, called on the owner of a small business that he thought could use his company's products. The owner seemed interested but didn't order. The next week, Jim called again with some additional information he had put together for the businessman, but he still wouldn't place an order.

The next week, Jim took a different approach. He walked in with an order form filled out for supplies that the business needed. Jim asked a few more questions to determine if there was anything else the owner needed. Then Jim handed him the completed form and said, "If you'll just sign here, I'll get this delivered to you today." The owner looked it over and signed it. Sometimes those who want to buy just don't want to make the decision alone.

What to Do When the Customer
14
RAISES OBSTACLES OR OBJECTIONS TO BUYING

The objective is not to defeat the prospect but
convince him that if he makes the purchase he's
going to be happier and better off as a result.

—DAN BELLUS

"I want to think it over."

"Your price is too high."

"We're already using [one of your competitor's products or services] and are very satisfied."

Sound familiar? If part of your job consists of selling, then you know that obstacles and objections come with the territory. In any given day you will get all sorts of reasons from customers who aren't willing to buy what you have to offer. Yet the bottom line to all obstacles and objections is this:

They don't value what you're selling as much as they value the money it costs.

As I pointed out in Chapter 4, people buy good feelings and solutions to problems. And when customers stall or raise objections, that's your cue to come up with more good feelings and solutions that will show them that your products and services are worth more to them than the money in their pocket. It's a simple concept but one that takes a lot of thought and preparation before the moment of truth and skillful application at the moment of truth. Here's the plan: Whenever a customer (or prospective customer) raises obstacles or objects to buying:

Reward by Agreeing, Empathizing, and Building Value

Whenever you encounter an objection or stall it's only natural to want to show the customer why he is wrong and that only an idiot would pass up the fantastic deal that you're offering him. But that's only going to make him mad and cost you a customer. Like the angry customer, the stalling or objecting customer has certain feelings and a point of view that must be dealt with first.

The next time a customer raises an obstacle or objection, begin by listening intently and *agreeing* with his point of view. I don't care how ridiculous or irrational it sounds to you. His point of view and his feelings are reality as he sees it, and until you convince him that you really want to see things his way, he won't be willing to try to see things your way. Nod your head in agreement when he gives you a reason for not buying and paraphrase his reason to let him know that you understand his point of view. Match his mood and tone of voice. The basic message you want to get across is, "I'm on your side. I understand how you feel and if I were in your shoes I would feel the same way." Empathic agreement is the first crucial step to melting obstacles and objections. The barriers to buying won't go away unless the customer feels that you really want to understand and help him.

Once you get in sync with the customer's feelings and point of view and establish rapport, he will likely listen to you. And that's your cue to start building value by explaining the many benefits of owning what you're offering. When the customer's perceived value of what you're selling is greater than his reasons for not buying, he will buy.

How to Remove Obstacles by Building Value

It's generally agreed by practicioners and students of selling that four major obstacles to buying must be removed before a sale takes place. (We are assuming that the customer has the resources to pay for what you are selling. Obviously, if he doesn't have the money or ability to finance the purchase, there can be no sale.) Those four obstacles are popularly known as the four no's of selling:

1. No trust. The customer doesn't trust you or believe what you are telling him. This obstacle must be removed first and foremost simply because customers will buy and continue to buy only from those whom they like and trust. He probably won't call you a liar but will ask something like, "How can I be sure that this will do everything you say it will?"

There are three basic steps to overcoming the no trust hurdle, and we have already covered two of them. First, practice the better than selling principle: Your basic purpose is to help people buy what's right for them and help them to get what they want. It's much easier to be perceived as trustworthy when you really are. Second, reward with empathic agreement, in the way that I mentioned earlier in this chapter. And third, let other satisfied customers speak for you. Furnish your prospective buyers with letters, names, addresses, and telephone numbers of satisfied customers who have used or are using what you have to offer. In my work as a professional speaker and seminar leader, I have found the testimony of satisfied customers to be one of the best value builders of all. In most cases, you encounter the no trust obstacle only with new customers.

2. No need. The second reason people don't buy is that they don't want or need what you have to offer. There's no point in selling snowballs to Eskimos or coconuts to Polynesians. Pushing your products and services on people who have no use for them is a waste of your time and will likely come back to haunt you. Spend your time seeking out and helping those who can actually benefit from what you're offering.

How do you tell if customers really have no need or if it's just a put-off? Use the problem-solving approach that was covered in Chapter 4. Ask probing questions to find out what the situation is now and what they would like it to be. If what they want is different from what they have, and you can help them, show them how. When you demonstrate how your products or services will get them what they want, you build value in the customers' minds. If you can't help, refer them to someone who can, and thank them for their time.

3. No help. The third obstacle to buying is that the customer is already using one of your competitor's products or services and doesn't believe that you can help him. This is where an intimate working knowledge of your competitor's strengths and weaknesses (as well as your own) can make a sale. Never knock a competitor. Instead, build value by pointing out the special benefits of buying what you have to offer.

For example, not long ago I went into a large electronics discount store. A young salesperson saw me admiring a new cordless telephone and said, "That's the finest cordless telephone on the market today, according to *Consumer Reports.*"

"It sure is nice, but I already have one." I replied. He asked what kind I had and I told him. "That's a fine telephone," he said, "but this model has a mute button, a hold button, ten memories, and a speaker phone with a dial built into the base." (My old cordless had none of these, and somehow this guy knew I was a gadget freak.) "It's like having two phones in one. A lot of cordless telephone pick up hum, but not this one. It sounds clear as a crystal. In fact, this is the model I'm going to buy when I can afford it."

Guess who's the proud owner of a new cordless telephone?

4. *No hurry.* "I want to think it over," is what you hear when you encounter this obstacle. The customer likes what you have to offer but not enough to buy today. And in many cases he really isn't going to think it over. He is going to forget about you and what you're selling unless you take appropriate action to remove the no hurry obstacle.

If people really want to think it over before buying, it's because they are afraid of making a buying decision that they will later regret. Consequently, your strategy is to minimize the risk of buying while maximizing the benefits for acting now. Offer them a money-back guarantee, offer a free trial period, and give them a special price or throw in something extra for buying today. As you reduce the risks of buying and increase the rewards for acting now, the no hurry obstacle will vanish. The Sharper Image's policies of offering a thirty-day money-back guarantee, refunding the difference if you see the product advertised at a lower price, and a toll-free number to handle any problems quickly (as mentioned in Chapter 6) is a classic example of how one company removes the no hurry obstacle.

Agreement, Empathy, and Building Value Melts Objections Too

Removing the four basic obstacles to a sale makes one possible but it's no guarantee of success. You still may encounter objections from the customer before he is ready to sign on the dotted line. The difference between an obstacle and an objection is that an objection is a definite statement of interest. In effect, the customer is telling you, "I like what you have to offer but we have to clear up some problems in my mind before I'm ready to buy."

Unfortunately most objections usually aren't expressed so pleasantly. Instead, you hear statements like, "It costs too much," "I can get a much better deal down the street," "I can't afford it," or "I don't like the color." Objections will cost you customers unless you're armed with the knowledge and preparation to deal with them. Here are several basic strategies you can use to handle objectives like a pro by rewarding the customer with agreement, empathy, and value.

1. *Anticipate objections and deal with them before the customer brings them up.* The best medicine is preventive medicine. The fewer the objections the customer raises, the greater are your chances for success. If you sell the same product or service frequently, you're bound to hear the same objections popping up time and again. If that's the case, decide how to deal with the objection and handle it while you're interviewing the customer or making your presentation. That way it never becomes an objection in the customer's mind.

For example, last year when I went car shopping, the salesperson looked at my six-year-old automobile and asked, "Do you plan on keeping your new car for six years?"

"Probably," I replied. With that, he proceeded to show me how for only a few dollars more per day I could be driving a Lincoln Continental that sold for about ten thousand dollars more than the model I went in to inquire about. Two days later, I bought a Continental. He never gave me a chance to say, "I can't afford it," or, "There's no way I'm ever going to pay that much for a car." He showed me that for only a relatively small amount of money each day I could spend the next several years riding around in the lap of luxury. In effect, he eliminated the price objection before I had a chance to raise it.

2. *"Never let 'em see you sweat."* That's the advice of a popular deodorant commercial and it's good advice for handling objections. You can't create a psychological oneness with the customer if you feel uncomfortable or on the defensive. Don't let objections shake you. Welcome them. It's a sign of interest. When the customer raises an objection, smile and nod in agreement. Treat it as a desire for more information, because that's precisely what an objection is. Then put the next idea to work.

3. *Use the feel, felt, found formula.* In his excellent book *The Best Seller!*, author and sales trainer Ron Willingham offers an effective,

easy-to-remember way to melt a customer's resistance and get him on your side. You can use this formula to deal with objections, put-offs, or even an unhappy customer. Here's how Willingham explains it:

> Whenever you get a negative response from people, take a deep breath, look them right in their eyeballs, and calmly say, "I understand how you *feel*. . . ." Then let them know that others *felt* the same way until they *found* out . . . (and here inject what they found out that changed their minds). This is one of the most disarming strategies that a salesperson can use.*

With the feel, felt, found formula, you can build value in the customer's mind without bruising his ego or putting him on the defensive. For example, not long ago I was in a car care center and heard a customer say, "The price of these steel-belted radial tires is highway robbery." Somewhat taken back, the salesperson replied, "Well, you get what you pay for. Good things aren't cheap and cheap things aren't good." The customer turned around and walked out.

A better way to handle it would have been to say, "I understand how you *feel*. They sure do cost a lot. My wife *felt* just like you do until I put a set on the family car. That's when she *found* out that they last twice as long, get better gas mileage, almost never go flat or blow out, and are a whole lot safer on wet pavement. Now she won't use anything else. She thinks the extra price is worth it just for the added safety and peace of mind."

Make it a habit to practice and use the feel, felt, found formula in your dealing with customers. It's one of the most valuable negotiating skills you can learn.

4. Translate features into benefits using the six magic words. Remember, people don't buy products or services. They buy what the products or services will do for them. Consequently, your job as a value builder is to tell the customer how he is going to benefit from what you're offering. So here's another excellent tip from Ron Willingham: Whenever you mention a feature, follow it up with six

*Ron Willingham, *The Best Seller!* (Englewood Cliffs, NJ: Prentice-Hall, Inc., 1984). p. 82.

magic words: *"What this means to you is . . ."* Then complete the sentence by explaining how the customer will benefit from the feature. For example:

> You're right. Our individual retirement accounts don't pay as high a rate as some. But our program has disability coverage. What this means to you is that if you ever have a lengthy illness or become disabled, we will make the maximum contribution to your IRA for you. You'll have the peace of mind of knowing that your retirement plan is secure.

> This is an expensive television but it comes with a five-year unconditional warranty on parts and labor. What this means to you is that you won't spend another penny on this set for at least the next five years. And in the unlikely event that the set breaks, we will furnish you with an equivalent one at no charge while yours is being repaired. Just pick up the phone and we will send someone out.

> Our customer service training program is a sizeable investment, but each participant receives a cassette program to reinforce the points covered. What this means to you is that you and your people will be able to listen time and again to the important lessons of how to win and keep customers. Through repeated learning, the techniques of quality customer service will become as natural as breathing and your business will prosper and grow.

As customers, we have all run into salespeople who rattle off features (such as megabytes, fuel injection, or BTUs) that mean absolutely nothing to us. Tell the customer in his words and in terms he understands what the feature will do for him. And one final point: Know your customer's wants well enough to understand what benefits are important to him. There's little point in talking about the benefits of fuel economy if the customer is interested in style or performance.

5. *Be alert for smoke screens and yes-but customers.* From time to time you're bound to run into customers who seem to have an endless list of objections. As soon as you answer one objection, they

raise another. When this happens, one of two things is going on. Either they aren't telling you their real objection, or they are playing the "yes-but" game with you. No matter how well you answer one objection, they will say, "Yes, but," and raise another. They aren't really interested in buying. A good sales transaction has two winners, but in this kind of game, nobody wins.

If you get repeated objections that you suspect are smoke screens or yes-but tactics, but a halt to it. Politely tell the customer something like: "Mrs. Johnson, I really want to clear up any misgivings you have about buying this. But are the objections you're raising the real reasons why you aren't ready to buy? Please tell me the real reason and give me a fair chance to answer it." If the customer raises another objection, preface your answer with, "If I answer this to your satisfaction, would you be willing to buy today?" By taking such an approach, you'll find out quickly if the customer is seriously interested in buying.

6. Let the customer experience the benefits of buying. What happens when you go into an ice cream parlor and ask about a new exotic flavor? That's right, the salesperson offers you a free taste. And more often than not, people buy the flavor they taste. The more customers can see, hear, touch, smell, taste, and feel how wonderful it is to buy what you sell, the more value they will perceive and the more likely it is they will buy.

When I went car shopping, the salesperson got me behind the wheel of a Continental so I could experience the smooth, quiet ride, the smell of new leather seats, the ease of handling, and all the luxurious appointments. I imagined myself gliding around town every day with the windows rolled up and the stereo playing soft music, thinking, "I wonder what the poor folks are doing." An old Chinese proverb says it best: "Tell me, I'll forget. Show me, I may remember. But involve me, and I'll understand."

If you can't let the customer actually experience all the benefits of buying, paint positive word pictures of the future benefits of buying what you're offering. Then paint negative word pictures of what he will miss by not buying. For example, if you sell houses, paint positive word pictures of his getting a healthy tax refund check each spring and living secure and rent-free in retirement, and of the satisfaction of having made a sound investment and the freedom and pride of home ownership. Then let him experience the loss of not buying. Paint negative word pictures of him shelling out more money to the government every April, paying rent every month that he will never see again, and possibly being evicted or not being able to pay rent in his later years. People are usually motivated more by the fear of loss than by the desire for gain. That's why the insurance industry is so big.

In his bestselling book, *Zig Ziglar's Secrets Of Closing The Sale,* Zig Ziglar presents a great recipe for overcoming the most common objection of all: "It costs too much." Ziglar's reply is:

> The price is high. I don't think there's any question about the price being high, Mr. Prospect, but when you add the benefits of quality, subtract the disappointments of cheapness, multiply the pleasure of buying something good, and divide the cost over a period of time, the arithmetic comes out in your favor. . . . If it costs you a hundred dollars but does you a thousand dollars worth of good, then by any yardstick you've bought a bargain, haven't you?*

Keep that formula in mind the next time you encounter an objection: Add the benefits of quality, subtract the disappointments of cheapness, multiply the pleasure of buying something good and divide the cost over the period of time that the customer will be using it. By doing that, you will be building value. And value, coupled with agreements and empathy, is what it takes to melt obstacles and objections.

---

*Zig Ziglar, *Zig Ziglar's Secrets Of Closing The Sale* (New York: Berkley Books, 1985), pp. 268–269.

15 What to Do When the Customer
GIVES BUYING SIGNALS

He who hesitates is last.

—MAE WEST

Samuel Clemens (aka Mark Twain) once told of going to a missionary meeting and becoming terribly impressed with the speaker's
religious zeal. At first, he decided to donate five dollars at collection
time, instead of his usual donation of one dollar. As the preacher
spoke on, Clemens became even more enthusiastic and decided to
write a large check to the missionary's charity. But instead of shut-
ting up and passing the plate, the preacher got carried away with the
sound of his own voice. And the longer he spoke, the more irritated
Clemens became at the man's lack of good judgment. Finally, when
the preacher passed the plate, Clemens was so steamed that instead
of making a contribution, he took out a dime.

It's all too common for salespeople to spend a half hour selling
their services and two hours buying them back. There's a time to
talk, a time to listen, and a time to close. And those who succeed at
winning and keeping customers know how to recognize, respond to,
and reward those moments of truth when the customer gives buying
signals. Whenever you recognize that a customer is giving definite
buying signals, that's your cue to do three things in the following
order:

- Reinforce the buying signal
- Make it easy to buy
- Ask for the business

Virtually everything you are about to read in this chapter is based on an obvious but often overlooked principle: *The best time to sell is when the customer is ready to buy.*

Many traditional salespersons and sales trainers will advise you to try closing "early and often." They reason that you never know when the customer is ready to buy, so you should ask him to buy at the earliest possible opportunity. I thoroughly disagree. Taking such a strategy will get you branded as a manipulative arm-twister whose sole purpose is to separate customers from their money. Furthermore, if you ask the customer to buy too soon and he says "no," it's going to be even more difficult to make him say "yes" later on. You should consider asking for business only after you have taken the time to establish a relationship of mutual trust and believe that you can help the customer get what he wants.

How to Recognize and Reinforce Buying Signals

In general, a buying signal is anything that a customer says or does that indicates enthusiasm or excitement about what you're offering. More specifically, below are some of the more common verbal and nonverbal buying signals.

VERBAL BUYING SIGNALS

- The customer asks such questions as, "Could I see that again?" "Would you go over that one more time?" "How soon can you get one for me?" "What other colors does it come in?"
- He agrees with what you're saying.
- He talks positively about what it would be like to own what you're offering.
- He answers your questions easily and positively.
- He wants more information, such as how much down payment is required or whether financing can be arranged.

NONVERBAL BUYING SIGNALS

- The customer leans slightly forward.
- He looks at you more.
- His eyes open up and twinkle or the pupils dilate slightly.
- He smiles and his brow is relaxed and unfurrowed.
- He nods in agreement with what you say.
- His lips are relaxed and open, rather than tight and drawn.
- His arms are relaxed and open and the palms of his hands are open toward you.
- His legs are uncrossed, or crossed facing toward you.
- He rests his hand on his chin or cheek or rubs his hands together.
- He handles or studies order forms or sales materials.
- He unconsciously reaches for his checkbook, wallet, or purse.
- He makes calculations on paper.
- He reaches for the sales contract.

Let's assume that you have a customer you can help, and that you are doing a good job of showing him how you can help him. Now is the time to put up your sensory antennae and start looking and listening for buying signals. Every time you explain a benefit of what you are offering, carefully observe the customer's behavior. If he responds indifferently, explain the next benefit. If he raises an objection, handle it in the manner we discussed in the previous chapter. Sometimes an objection is a buying signal. But if he responds with a buying signal, reward it with your approval and get ready to close. Smile and nod. Make a rewarding comment, such as, "I'm glad you asked that" or "You're very wise to base your buying decision on quality and value, rather than the lowest price." Signify with your words and your behavior that you like what he is doing or saying and the odds are he will continue to repeat the behavior and buy.

Although there may be literally dozens of reasons why the customer should buy what you offer, he usually buys for only one or two reasons. Once you explain a benefit that brings forth a buying signal, there's no need to keep explaining other benefits. Keep the buying decision simple for the customer. You've found the hot button and it's time to start closing.

Make It Easy to Buy

Once the customer decides that he wants to buy, he is confronted with a whole new set of problems, such as:

* How will I pay for it?
* Where will I put it?
* What if it doesn't work out?
* What if it breaks?
* How can I justify it to my spouse or boss?

In short, most customers go into the scared emotional state before making the final buying decision. And if you don't take steps to eliminate that fear, you'll likely lose the sale. Ask the customer, "Does all of this make sense to you? It really fits your needs and I don't want you to pass it up because I haven't done a good enough job of explaining what it will do for you." This is a nonthreatening way to get the customer to open up and it takes the burden off of him for not understanding.

If he still has a problem, handle it like an objection, because that's what it is. Reassure him that he can afford it with your convenient financing plan. Reemphasize your money-back, no-questions-asked guarantee. Give him ideas for places he can put it. Your spouse loves the one you bought and his will too. Can you offer him a free trial period? (Apple Computer sold a lot of Macintoshes by letting customers take one home overnight.) Show him how others justified the investment to their bosses. And as a clincher, throw in something extra or give him a special price for acting now. In summary, you make it easy to buy by giving him *reasons* for buying what he *wants* to buy, and by doing whatever you can to take the risk and worry out of the buying decision. As Paul Parker put it, "People like to feel they are buying their own good judgment as a result of the information that the salesman has given them."

Closing Is Asking for the Business

If you have established rapport with your customer, decided you can help him and shown him how, received buying signals, and removed the worry and risk from the buying decision, there's only one thing left to do: Tactfully ask for the order. "May I order one for you?" "Can we choose a delivery date?" "How many would you like?" "Try it. You'll like it." You don't need 101 sure-fire closes to manipulate people into buying if you have completed the preceding steps. **But you do have to ask for the order!**

Incredible as it seems, almost two-thirds of all sales calls conclude without the salesperson asking for the order. Yet it's one of the most crucial ingredients to winning and keeping customers. You may offer the greatest products and services and have the greatest marketing strategy in the world. But unless you cultivate the habit of asking for the order, you're going to lose a lot of business.

The best time to ask is when people are picturing the benefits of using what you're selling. Summarize the key benefits that appeal to the customer most before asking. Then, look him in the eye, ask him to buy, and don't say anything until he answers. Waiting until you get a buying signal and making it easy to buy greatly increases the odds of your getting a "yes" when you ask for the order.

In the event that you do get a refusal, it will likely come in the form of an objection. If that's the case, handle it and ask again. If you get another objection, handle it and ask again. When it comes to success in selling, tactful persistence in the face of rejection is the name of the game. If you doubt that, consider the following statistics: of those salespersons who ask for the order:

- 44 percent give up after one "no."
- 22 percent give up after two "no's."
- 14 percent give up after three "no's."
- 12 percent give up after four "no's."

If you add up those percentages, you get 92 percent of all salespersons giving up without asking for the order a fifth time. This leaves only 8 percent of all salespersons who will ask for the order more than four times. But consider this: *Sixty percent of all customers say "no" four times before saying "yes."* The obvious inference is that 8 percent of the salespeople are getting 60 percent of the business just by being hard-headed enough to keep asking. Author and sales trainer Hank Trisler put it best:

Here's the real key to selling. *You ask, you get.* The more you ask, the more you get. If you don't ask you don't get. You can go to all the seminars that come to your town, read all the books, listen to all the tapes. If you don't learn to ask, you're going to go broke.*

The next time you get discouraged with a customer's refusal, consider this: Water is only an idle liquid at 211 degrees but boils into a full head of steam at 212. Just one small degree makes a tremendous difference. Much the same is true in selling. Asking one more time can be the difference between winning and losing a sale. In the final analysis, either the customer buys or he doesn't. Coming close only counts in horseshoes and dancing.

Recognizing and rewarding buying signals is much more an art than a science and has to be tailored to your personality, the customer you're dealing with, and the situation. It's like most things—you'll get better with practice. But if you make a conscious effort to reinforce buying signals, make it easy to buy, and ask for the order, chances are you'll be well on your way to the next moment of truth.

*Hank Trisler, *No Bull Selling* (New York: Bantam Books, 1985), p. 145.

16

What to Do When the Customer

BUYS

There's no traffic jam on the extra mile.

—ANONYMOUS

Lagniappe. That word (pronounced lan-yap) probably means nothing to you—unless you happen to live in southern Louisiana. It means "something extra" and has its origins many years ago with Creole shopkeepers. For example, if a customer asked for five pounds of sugar, the shopkeeper would carefully scoop five pounds of sugar onto the scale. Then, with a smile, he would add an extra amount to the customer's order and say, "lagniappe," which was his way of saying, "I'm giving you your money's worth and a little bit more." Or, if a customer ordered several commodities, the shopkeeper might throw in a pound of bacon or some other small gift as lagniappe. It was a congenial way of building loyalty by giving the customer more than he asked for. Isn't it ironic that some two hundred years later, with all of our sophisticated research, we have come to the same conclusion that Creole shopkeepers had arrived at intuitively: *You win and keep customers by exceeding their expectations.*

Some years ago, I heard a sales trainer tell his audience that the sale begins when the customer says "no." While that may be an old motivational bromide for persistence, I believe that the sale really begins when the customer says "yes." It's how you perform after the customer buys that determines whether you *keep* him. And remember, it's a whole lot easier and more profitable to keep the customers you have than it is to win new ones. People prefer to buy from those that they already know. Consequently, when the customer buys, your basic strategy is to:

Reward Buying by Delivering More Than You Promise

The surest way to make customers fall in love with your business, come back for more, and tell others how wonderful you are is to practice the "and then some" principle. Your products do all that you said they would do—and then some. Your service is as prompt, reliable, and courteous as you promised it would be—and then some. If the customer needs help after the sale, you provide that help—and then some. It's the willingness to go that extra mile that separates the true champions from the also-rans. As former IBM vice-president Buck Rodgers put it, "It's what you offer over and above the basic product and how you perform that builds a solid business."

Lest you think that this is some pie-in-the-sky platitude that's designed to make you work harder for the same amount of money, consider this: Author Napoleon Hill devoted over twenty-five years of his life to trying to discover why so few men succeed and so many fail. He interviewed and studied the lives of numerous great achievers from all walks of life (such as Andrew Carnegie, Thomas Edison, and Woodrow Wilson) and presented the essence of his findings in his classic bestselling book, *Think and Grow Rich*. One of Hill's best recommendations is to cultivate the habit of rendering more and better service than that for which you are paid.

He recommended this for two reasons: First, it puts you head and shoulders above the competition because the sad truth is that most people provide only the minimum service required. No matter what you do, if you provide more of it and do it better than anyone else, the competition for your services will be keen. The greatest economic security in the world is to find something to do that people are willing to pay for and do it extremely well.

Second, it will build you an outstanding reputation and you will be able to command more money for your services. As Hill put it, "Make it your habit to render more service and better service than that for which you are paid, and lo! before you realize what has happened, you will find that THE WORLD IS WILLINGLY PAYING YOU FOR MORE THAN YOU DO!" Today, we call that building "perceived value." Fifty years ago, Napoleon Hill called it the "law of increasing returns." Two hundred years ago, Creole shopkeepers called it "lagniappe." No matter what you call it, the message is the same: If you want to be prosperous, give customers their money's worth—and then some.

When You Go That Extra Mile, Take These Steps

1. Reinforce the buying decision immediately. The sooner the customer feels rewarded for buying from you, the greater are the odds he will buy again. As soon as the customer says "yes" to your offer, reassure him that he's doing the right thing. Compliment his decision and tell him something like, "Great. I know you'll be glad you bought it." Then, throw in something extra as a reward for buying. For example, as soon as I agreed to buy my new car, the salesperson informed me that he would give me three years of free road service at no extra charge. Summarize the transaction, clear up any points that may be unclear in the customer's mind, and tell him what will happen next. Then check to see if there is anything else that you sell that may be of help to him. The law of inertia applies to customers too. Customers who buy tend to keep buying.

Later that day, write the customer a letter (preferably handwritten) thanking him for buying from you and telling him that his satisfaction is your top priority. Leave the customer with the impression that he is yours for keeps. I don't care how small the order is. Your goal is to establish a continuing relationship. Let him know that he can count on your help any time he has a need or problem— and mean it. After buying, most customers get a letter from the seller only when a payment is past due or they are trying to sell something else. Show the customer that you're different. You have class and you care.

2. Keep tabs on the order to insure that the customer gets what you promised. Once the order is placed, make sure that the internal arrangements are handled properly. Was the order processed correctly? Was the product or service shipped or delivered on time? Was the billing accurate and timely? Staying on top of the details will help you spot and correct any problems before they occur.

3. Make a nonselling follow-up call. This will really set you apart from the competition. As I pointed out earlier, most businesses don't bother to ask customers the platinum questions. They prefer to whistle in the dark and hope all is well, rather than taking the time to find out if the customer is truly satisfied. Call the customer and ask if everything is okay. Was it delivered on time? Is it working okay? Is he happy with it? Is he pleased with the service? Does he have any suggestions for improvement or ideas on how you can serve him better? If you can think of a new use for something that he bought, call him and tell him. If you have a minor gift or an accessory that will make what he bought more useful, send it to him with your compliments. Send a cookbook to the customer who just bought that new microwave oven or a special folder for keeping important papers to the person who just purchased an insurance policy. Writing a thank-you letter *tells* the customer that his satisfaction is important to you. Making a follow-up call *shows* him.

4. Keep good records and stay in touch. As I pointed out in the previous chapter, the best time to sell is when the customer is ready to buy. Regularly touch base with your customers to test for future business. Keep a written record of what each customer buys and when he buys it. Does he regularly reorder certain things at a certain time? When does his new budget begin? Does he have any new problems or opportunities on the horizon where you may be able to help? By keeping a record on each customer, you will be able to know when he is most in need of what you offer.

5. Turn your customers into goodwill ambassadors. An old saying has it that nothing sells better than a satisfied customer. That's only partly true, because most satisfied customers won't tell anybody about what great service you give *unless you ask them to.* Every time you get a satisfied customer, ask him to write a testimonial letter, on his stationery, stating how happy he is with your products or services. Get as many letters as you can from as many different regions and industries as possible. Potential buyers are more likely to believe testimonials from their industry or region of the country. If your customer doesn't know what to say, show him other testimonials or ask him a few questions about what he liked best. Then compose a sample letter for him. Given a working model, most customers will have no trouble writing a great testimonial in their own words. Similarly, ask your customers if you may use them as references for future customers.

And be sure to ask your satisfied customers for referrals. Get the names of two or three other persons or businesses that the customer feels could benefit from what you offer. When he gives you a name, ask for additional information about why he feels you could help this person. From what he tells you, you can decide if it's a prospect worth pursuing. Most truly satisfied customers will be delighted to give you referrals, and a high percentage of those referrals will become new customers.

Once a customer decides to buy, he is ultimately going to feel rewarded or regretful, and it's your job to help him feel the former. Go beyond the call of duty. Anything that sells a customer on you will eventually sell more products and services and keep on selling them. Get interested in your customers as people. Make an extra effort to solve their problems and make them feel good. You'll find it personally rewarding because your customers will become more than customers. They will become your friends.

*If you want a place in the sun, you've got to put
up with a few blisters.*

—ABIGAIL VAN BUREN

Jeff, a department store salesperson, spent the better part of an hour showing blankets to a customer. He repeatedly climbed a ladder, taking down blanket after blanket from the shelves. Finally, when there was only one blanket left, the customer shrugged her shoulders and said, "Oh, well, I really don't want to buy a blanket today. I'm just looking for a friend." Jeff sighed and replied, "Madam, if you really think she's in that one remaining blanket, I'll be glad to take it down for you."

No matter how wonderful you and your products and services are, there will be plenty of times when people will simply refuse to buy. Refusals can be frustrating, immobilizing, painful, and career-destroying, if you choose to let them be. On the other hand, refusals can be character-building lessons that point the way to future successes. In one sense, refusals are like knives. They can help or hurt you, depending on whether you grab them by the handle or the blade. It's all in how you choose to think and behave when the customer says no. Regardless of how you feel, whenever a customer refuses to buy:

Reward Refusals with Polite Appreciation

As frustrating as it may seem at the moment, this is your chance to make a friend who may buy later or refer you to someone who will. It's also your chance to find out why the customer chose not to buy, and to review your own behavior and learn from it. If you make a concerted effort to generate goodwill, learn from the experience, and keep trying, your future success at winning and keeping customers is virtually guaranteed.

If you want to be successful at anything in life, here's one of the most valuable pieces of information that I can give you: **Focusing on long-term goals will keep you from becoming sidetracked by short-term frustrations.** In school, business, marriage, childrearing, or any endeavor, the pathways of success are almost always marked with numerous frustrations and setbacks. For example, here are a few "failures" you may not have heard of:

- A young man's lifelong dream was to attend West Point. He was twice turned down but applied a third time and was accepted. His name was Douglas MacArthur.
- In the first year of operation, The Coca-Cola Company sold a measly four hundred Cokes.
- Both Hewlett-Packard and Atari turned down the opportunity to buy the first Apple microcomputer. First-year sales of the Apple were $2.5 million.
- Henry Ford went bankrupt in his first year in the automobile business and two years later his second company failed. His third one has done rather well.
- Twenty-three publishers rejected a children's book written by an author who called himself Dr. Seuss. The twenty-fourth publisher published it and the book sold six million copies.
- In 1903 King Gillette invented the safety razor and sold a grand total of 51 razors and 168 blades for the entire year.
- A dry-goods merchant went broke with his first three stores before the fourth one caught on. His name was R. H. Macy.

Talk to any successful person in almost any endeavor, and he can tell you about scores of frustrating experiences along the way. It's all just part of the price of success. As inventor Charles Kettering put it, "Failures, *repeated* failures, are finger posts on the road to achievement. The only time you don't fail is the last time you try something and it works. One *fails* toward success.

In boxing, a knockout is rarely the result of one punch. Instead, it's the cumulative effect of a series of blows that gets the final result. In football, it often seems that winning is the result of one or two big plays. But any coach will tell you that many more games are won with time-consuming drives and defenses that slowly wear the opponent down. Grand slam home runs in baseball are exciting, but a lot more games are won with base hits and consistent pitching. Similarly, your long-term success at winning and keeping customers isn't likely to result from rare, spectacular performances, but rather from consistent effort in the face of adversity. According to McGraw-Hill Research, it takes an average of 5.5 visits before a customer will say yes to a major sale.

When the Customer Says No, Keep These Points in Mind

1. Make every moment of truth count. You can't always make a sale but you can always make some progress toward your ultimate goal of winning and keeping customers. For example:

- You can ask prospects if you may be of help in the future.
- You can schedule another appointment.
- You can get information to find out if they would be a good customer for you.
- You can ask them for referrals.
- You can learn from any mistakes that you may have made.
- You can always leave a good impression.

Never leave a customer without having achieved at least one of those goals.

2. Think long term and keep the big picture in mind. It's not the customers you lose but the ones you win and keep that count. In reality, there's no such thing as a lost sale. How can you lose what you never had? You either win or break even, and those are much better odds than you can get in Las Vegas. As author Louis L'Amour put it, "Victory is won not in miles but in inches. Win a little now, hold your ground, and later win a little more."

Look at it this way: If you make one sale for every ten customers you talk to, and your average commission per sale is one hundred dollars, that's ten dollars per customer contact. The great author and playwright George Bernard Shaw wrote, "When I was young I observed that nine out of every ten things I did were failures, so I did ten times more work." Take a similar approach and you'll find yourself winning and keeping more customers than ever.

3. Don't take refusals personally or let them immobilize you. When the customer says no, it's not you that's being rejected. The offer and the customer just weren't right for each other, as the customer perceived it, and that's too bad. But that's all it is and there is no point in mentally beating yourself up about it.

When the customer says no, don't rush off. Ask him, "Why not?" That will force him to give you a reason for not buying, and when he thinks about it, he may change his mind. Or he may give you an objection that you can answer that will cause him to change his mind. Take the time to see if he has use for anything else that you're offering.

If he still doesn't buy, smile and do what you can to leave a good impression. You don't know how close he was to buying and you want to leave him with only pleasant memories. Sometimes the customer is checking you out to see what type of person you are. He wants time to mull over the ideas you presented to him or make sure that he can trust you. When you part company, thank him for his time and say something like, "I'm sorry I can't help you today, but I enjoyed talking with you. And I hope you'll give me the chance to help you in the future." Then promptly turn your attention to the next problem or customer and get absorbed in it. This will keep you from wasting time, getting depressed, and becoming immobilized over a customer's refusal.

Whatever you do, *don't let your disappointment show*. Remember, emotions are contagious and this customer or future ones aren't likely to buy if you carry a look of disaster on your face. Business is business. It's not a United Way campaign and very few people are going to buy from you because they feel sorry for you. People like to buy from winners who make them feel like winners. The single best thing you can do when things are tough is keep smiling. As Lucille Ball put it, "One of the things I learned the hard way was that it doesn't pay to get discouraged. Keeping busy and making optimism a way of life can restore your faith in yourself."

4. Resolve to learn something from every refusal. Every person who says no can provide you with valuable feedback. It isn't failure. It's a lesson. When the customer says no and you ask him why, you have already taken the first step.

While there is no point in feeling bad about a no, take the time to review each refusal contact and learn from it. Then use what you learn to help you perform better with future customers. Some of the things you may want to consider are:

- Were you prepared with a thorough knowledge of your products or services?
- Did you take the time to really listen and find out the customer's needs and wants? Did you match your product or service's benefits to his needs and wants?
- Did you stress the benefits that the customer would receive from buying and speak to him in his own language?
- What kind of impression did you make? Were you prompt, attentive, and well groomed? Was your presentation professional?
- Did you argue with the customer, exaggerate benefits, knock the competition, or try to pressure him into buying? Can you think of anything that you said or did that might have turned him off?
- How did you ask for the order? Did you handle his objections properly before asking? Did you wait for buying signals? Did you ask several times? Did you ask at all?
- Were you friendly and polite after he said no? Did you ask to be of help in the future? Did you ask for referrals? Did you leave him feeling glad that he talked with you?

Review the above checklist whenever a customer says no. The best performers in any endeavor continually monitor their performance in hopes of finding ways to get better. Regardless of what you do for a living, if you work at getting better every day, someday you'll be outstanding.

Similarly, if a customer calls and cancels an order, don't just accept it at face value. Try to find out why. Did he get a better price elsewhere? If so, maybe you can make him a better offer. Did he get poor service on a previous order? Perhaps you can make it up to him and see that the problem doesn't occur again. Have his needs changed? Maybe you can offer him something else that will suit him better.

5. *Cultivate the habit of intelligent persistence.* In the words of W. C. Fields, "If at first you don't succeed, try, try again. Then quit. No use being a damn fool about it." While you should never abandon your ultimate goal of winning and keeping customers, there are times when giving up on a particular prospect makes good sense. While I don't advocate giving up easily, there's a fine line between persistence and foolishness.

How long should you try before giving up on a prospect? I can't give you a specific answer because each situation is different. But here is a tip that will help you decide whether to persevere. Ask yourself, "Is continuing to pursue this prospect the best use of my time?" Even if the prospect eventually buys, the cost of perseverance may be too high. Time is money and the time spent with a difficult prospect might be better spent talking with more qualified prospects or existing customers. Weigh your investment of time against the potential long-term payoff and ask yourself, "Is it worth it?" More often than not, you'll find that the difficult prospect isn't the best use of your time. If that's the case, politely thank him, learn from the experience, and move on.

The most successful people at winning and keeping customers hear a whole lot more no's than yes's. But they have become winners because they realize that the way to become a winner is to make it okay to lose. And they practice the famous Winston Churchill formula for success: "Never, never, never quit."

What to Do When the Customer
18
COMPLAINS

A customer who complains is my best friend.

—STEW LEONARD

Bob sent a floral arrangement to Janet to celebrate the grand open-ing of her firm's new branch office. When he arrived at the grand opening, he was shocked to find out that the florist had delivered a wreath with an inscription reading "Rest in peace." But when he angrily complained to the florist, the reply was, "That's not so bad. Look at it this way: Somewhere a person was buried today under a wreath that read, 'Good luck in your new location.' "

If you or your business treat customer complaints like the florist did, you're overlooking a tremendous opportunity. Seeking out and identifying customer complaints is one of the most potentially profit-able activities that a business can engage in. That conclusion was reached in a 1986 study done by the federal Office of Consumer Affairs. In fact, some companies, such as General Electric, General Motors, Polaroid, and American Express, have initiated innovative programs to seek out and resolve customer complaints. The pro-grams include toll-free hotlines for customers, identifying root causes of complaints, and teaching employees to deal with angry customers. According to the study, the programs are providing a return on investment ranging anywhere from 15 to 400 percent.

Customer complaint programs pay off handsomely for three basic reasons:

1. *Complaints point out areas that need improvement.* It's one way of finding answers to the platinum questions "How are we doing?" and "How can we get better?" While complaints may not be the most positive of messages, smart companies and employees learn to gather and use complaint information to identify weak spots and take corrective action. A business that doesn't know how or where it needs to improve is no better off than one that can't.

2. *Complaints give you a second chance to provide service and satisfaction to dissatisfied customers.* Remember, a typical business hears from only 4 percent of its dissatisfied customers. That means that the remaining 96 percent are "nice customers" who probably aren't going to give you a second chance. They're just going to smile, take their business elsewhere, and tell their friends about the lousy service you give. On the other hand, a complaining customer is being honest with you and giving you another opportunity to make good. Now I ask you: Who are your true friends, the complainers or the "nice customers"?

3. *Complaints are a wonderful opportunity to strengthen customer loyalty.* Right or wrong, most customers don't think about what kind of service you give when everything goes well. They simply take it for granted. But when there's a problem, you can rest assured that they are thinking about you and your service—a lot. And that's your chance to really show them just what great service you give and that you're willing to do whatever is reasonably possible to see that they are satisfied. Remember, 70 percent of complaining customers will buy from you again if you resolve the problem in their favor, and 95 percent will buy again if you resolve the problem on the spot. Consequently, the most important thing to remember is to:

Reward Complaints with Fast, Positive Action

A rapidly settled complaint can actually create more customer loyalty than would have been created if it had never occurred. Customers are much more likely to remember the "extra touch," fast action, and genuine concern that you exhibited when they felt dissatisfied. On the other hand, a mishandled complaint can cost you much, much more than a customer. In addition to bad-mouthing your company, customers who feel mistreated have been known to sue. And many a business has had the misfortune of seeing, hearing, and reading about a dissatisfied customer in the media. That's one kind of publicity no business can afford.

Some General Guidelines for Handling Complaints

Complaining customers can be a gold mine of future business or a blueprint for disaster, depending largely on how you reward them at the moment of truth. We will get to the specifics of handling customer complaints at the moment of truth shortly. But first, here are some general guidelines about complaints that every business and every employee needs to understand.

1. Seek out and welcome complaints. They aren't annoyances but opportunities to get better and build customer loyalty. Be wary of long-term customers who never complain. Nobody is ever totally satisfied for an extended period of time. Either they aren't being candid or they aren't being asked the platinum questions.

2. Take every complaint seriously. An old proverb says that only the wearer knows how badly the shoe pinches. There is no such thing as a small complaint. What seems minor to you may loom very large in the customer's mind. Consider every complaint as a serious opportunity that you cannot afford to overlook.

3. Get people at the top actively involved in both listening to and helping resolve customer complaints. This is an excellent way for top management to learn customer wants and then respond with action to meet those wants. Too many managers make decisions in a vacuum without understanding the needs and wants of the customers who make the business possible.

4. Consider setting up a system to document and classify complaints. This will help you spot the greatest areas of customer irritation that need immediate action. For example, you may want to have a complaint log to document when a complaint is received, what it is, and how and when it was resolved. Or you may find it useful to create a one-page complaint form for handling each complaint. Some items you might want to record on the form are:

- The customer's name, address, and telephone number
- The name of the employee receiving the complaint
- The date and time the complaint was received and resolved

- The nature of the complaint
- The mutually agreed solution to the problem
- Whether the problem was resolved on the spot
- If not, when a solution was promised to the customer
- What steps have to be taken
- How this problem could have been prevented
- What can be done to prevent this problem in the future
- The date and time that the customer was contacted to insure that the problem has been solved and that he is satisfied
- What, if anything, was done (or should be done) to compensate the customer for his inconvenience

Depending on your business, some of the above items may not be necessary. You may not need a complaint form at all or may want to use one only infrequently to sample the nature of your complaints. If you feel a complaint form is valuable for your business, construct one that can be filled out as simply and quickly as possible. Questions with "check 'yes' or 'no'" and multiple-choice answers are the most quickly and easily answered. You want a system for gathering the most crucial information with the least possible red tape.

5. *Set goals for resolving complaints.* For example, you may want to set such goals as calling back 90 percent of all customers who complain within an hour or resolving 65 percent of all complaints on the spot, or any goal whose achievement will turn customer complaints into an asset rather than a liability. Setting specific, measurable goals for resolving complaints increases the odds that more of them will be handled satisfactorily.

6. *Learn and get better from complaints.* In addition to pointing out ways that the quality of service can be improved, studying and analyzing complaints can reveal all sorts of unexpected findings. For example, in analyzing policyholder complaints, State Farm Insurance found that 70 percent of all complaints were caused by faulty communication. This pointed out the need for greater employee training in complaint handling and the need for a broader exposure to effective communications concepts.

Specifics for the Moments of Truth

On the subject of complaint handling, Theo Mitchelson, deputy regional vice-president of State Farm Insurance, writes, "when things go wrong they (customers) don't want to communicate with an 'organization' or a computer. They want to talk with a real, live, responsive person . . . a responsible person who will listen and help them get satisfaction. Consumers not only want quality, but they want a meaningful dialogue with the people they do business with."

Inasmuch as many of your complaining customers will also be angry or upset, what we covered in Chapter 11 often applies to those who complain. Reacting helpfully rather than defensively, keeping your cool, and listening with empathy and for the facts will always help you in resolving customer complaints. More specifically, here are some tips for handling complaints.

1. Listen with understanding. It defuses anger and demonstrates your concern. Tell the customer something like, "I'm sorry you have been inconvenienced. Tell me what happened so I can help you." The vital thing is to show a sincere interest and willingness to help. The customer's first impression of you is all-important in gaining cooperation.

No matter what caused the problem, don't blame others or make excuses. An excuse is a reason with a bad reputation. Take full responsibility for fixing the problem and do whatever you can to solve it as rapidly as possible.

2. Paraphrase and record what the customer tells you. Whenever you hear an important point, say something like, "Let me make sure I have this straight, you were promised delivery on the fifteenth and didn't get it until the first of the following month. Is that correct? Let me make a note of that."

3. Find out what the customer wants. Does he want a refund? A credit? A discount? A replacement? He is complaining because he has a problem and wants it solved as quickly as possible. Find out what it is.

4. Propose a solution and get his support. When you have found out what the customer wants, a solution is usually obvious. State your solution in a positive manner. "I'll be happy to take it back and give you full credit for it on other merchandise. Is that okay with you?" If it is, act quickly.

5. If the customer doesn't like your solution, ask him what he would consider a fair settlement. Only a small percentage (10 percent or less) of complaining customers will be unreasonable. No matter what you do, this irrational group will never be satisfied, because they complain for the sake of complaining. If that's the case, just politely offer them a refund and send them on their way. But most people have a reasonable sense of what is fair, and quite often they will propose an equitable solution. If you feel the customer's request is reasonable and you have the authority to handle it, do it now. If you don't have the authority to grant the request, contact someone who can and get permission—now.

6. *Make a follow-up call to insure satisfaction.* Where appropriate, call the customer back at a later date to make sure that he is satisfied. This will achieve two things. First, it will verify that the problem has been taken care of. And second, it will leave the customer with a positive final impression about your desire to give good service. Right or wrong, customers will remember their final contact with you the most. The last impression is the lasting impression.

7. *Never let the customer lose face.* If you cannot meet a customer's expectations, politely tell him without delay. But never tell a customer that he is wrong and never allow yourself to be drawn into an argument. As with most customer contact situations, it is vital to be courteous and considerate of his feelings and to listen. Sometimes customers know full well that there is nothing you can do. All they really want is someone to hear them out and respect their point of view. And you can always give them that.

Years ago, a passenger in a railway car absentmindedly wrote "chicken sandwich" on an order slip when ordering a chicken salad sandwich. When the waiter brought a chicken sandwich, the passenger complained that he had ordered chicken salad. Instead of showing him the order slip, the waiter expressed his regret, politely picked up the sandwich, and returned shortly thereafter with a chicken salad sandwich.

While eating the sandwich, the customer picked up the order slip and realized that the mistake was his. He called the waiter, apologized, and offered to pay for both sandwiches. But the waiter's reply was, "No, sir. That's perfectly all right. I'm just happy you've forgiven me for being right."

It may be a cliché, but "The customer is always right" is a policy that still wins and keeps customers.

19

What to Do When the Customer

IS GOING TO BE DISAPPOINTED

Feelings are everywhere—be gentle.

—J. MASAI

A soldier stationed overseas phoned home. His brother answered and promptly told him, "Your cat fell off the roof and died."

"That's a terrible way to break bad news," the soldier replied. "You didn't have to hit me with it so suddenly. Bad news should be broken to people gradually. For example, you could have begun by telling me that the cat was playing on the roof. Then you could have mentioned that he got too close to the edge. Then you could have said that he fell off the roof and was injured. And then you could have said that you rushed him to the vet but he died later from the injuries."

"Gee, I'm sorry." said the brother.

"That's OK," replied the soldier. "At least you'll know better next time. How's Mom?"

After a long pause the brother answered, "She's playing on the roof."

There will be times when, like the soldier, your customers are in for bad news. It probably won't be nearly as drastic as the "Mom's playing on the roof" variety, but it will be disappointing. For example:

- You can't complete the job at the time it was promised.
- What you thought was a minor problem is a major one and the cost exceeds the estimate you gave the customer.
- The customer misunderstood what your product or service would do for him and is expecting more than you can deliver.
- Being only human, you or someone else made mistakes that will inconvenience the customer.

An old Turkish proverb advises that the messenger with bad news should always keep one foot in the stirrup. When you realize that the customer is going to be disappointed, it's only normal to not want to give him the bad news. But it's also the worst possible thing you can do. It's far better to tell the customer and take heat than it is to keep him in the dark and ultimately lose him.

Whenever things go wrong that will affect the customer, let him know immediately. While the message may be initially disappointing, keeping customers informed builds the confidence and trust necessary for a continuing relationship. On the other hand, letting the customer find out the bad news for himself magnifies and multiplies the disappointment.

For example, have you ever taken your car to a dealership for repairs, gone to the trouble and expense of taking a taxi to pick it up at the promised time, and then been told that it wouldn't be ready until tomorrow? How did that make you feel? It's bad enough that the car isn't ready, but these jokers think it's too much trouble to pick up the phone and tell you. Scratch one customer.

But, on the other hand, let's assume that the dealer calls and tells you, "I know that we promised you that your car would be ready this evening, but we ran into some unexpected problems. We will have your car ready by noon tomorrow at the latest. I'm sorry for this inconvenience. As soon as it's ready we will call you." While you may be disappointed, at least you're being spared the time and expense of taking a taxi. And you know that they are thinking about you. But even better, let's assume the dealer adds, "If you need a car, we will be happy to lend you one of our loaner cars overnight at no charge. Can we drop one off to you?" Now, how do you feel about the dealership? Assuming that you're not in shock (I would have passed out!), chances are that your feelings would be very positive. And that's why whenever you have to give a customer disappointing news:

Reward with Positive Perks

Do something special for the customer to offset the hurt. As I mentioned earlier, customers exchange their money for good feelings and the expectation of good feelings. And when customers are disappointed they think, "That's not fair. I pay these people to solve my problems and now they are creating problems for me." In other words, when you give a customer disappointing news, you are making a withdrawal from their emotional bank account. Consequently, it's important to make a deposit to offset, or at least minimize, the withdrawal.

For example, I was recently dining at TGI Friday's and noticed that my meal was taking much longer than normal to arrive. I inquired about it and when the meal came the waiter said, "I'm sorry this took so long. We won't charge you for it." Doing that something extra for the inconvenienced customer leaves a positive impression about your quality of service.

Similarly, National Bank of Detroit offered to pay customers ten dollars for each error they discover in their checking accounts. Not surprisingly, after making this offer known, the bank picked up fifteen thousand new accounts and $65.5 million in deposits in the following two months. And First Union National Bank of Charlotte, North Carolina, sends a dozen roses to customers who have been badly inconvenienced or whose accounts are messed up. It's clear that First Union understands both financial and emotional banking.

In addition to doing something special for the disappointed or inconvenienced customer, here are two other ideas to keep in mind.

1. When things go wrong, apologize and take total responsibility for setting things straight. Don't criticize the company or other employees or make excuses. The customer doesn't want reasons. He wants results. To the customer, *you* are the company and when you run down the company you are only putting yourself down. If you know how a mishap can be prevented, don't tell the customer. Tell the people where you work who can do something about it. Let the customer know that mishaps like this are not regular occurrences in your organization and that you're willing to do whatever it takes to set things straight.

2. Remember that how people react to bad news depends largely on how you tell them. As my friend Mark Sanborn says, "You can't always tell people what they want to hear but you can tell them in such a way that they will want to listen." Nothing turns a customer off faster than giving him a flat "no" or bad news at the outset. Be positive and try to phrase your message by telling the customer what you can do for him. Set a positive tone at the outset. For example:

- If the model that a customer ordered has been discontinued, don't tell him, "I can't get it for you." Instead, tell him why the new model is better than the one he ordered.
- If you can't keep an 11:00 A.M. appointment, don't call and say "I can't come at eleven." Instead say something like, "Some problems have come up and I would like to come at three this afternoon or another time that's convenient for you. I apologize for the delay and hope this doesn't inconvenience you too much."
- If the washer, television, car, or whatever is beyond repair and you initially thought you could fix it, don't say, "I can't fix your washer. I'm a repairman, not a faith healer." Instead say, "The problem is more serious than I expected. It's such an expensive job to repair it that you may want to consider getting a new one."
- When the bill exceeds your original estimate, don't say, "This is going to cost you much more than I thought." Instead, explain what you had based the original estimate on and why the cost turned out to be higher. Point out that your estimate was just an estimate and not a written guarantee. And whenever possible, get the customer's permission before performing a job that exceeds the estimate.
- If a customer's disappointment is caused by his misunderstanding, don't say, "You just didn't understand that your children weren't covered by this policy." Instead say something like, "I'm sorry for this misunderstanding. To prevent this from happening again, I suggest that we go over all of your policies in detail together."

Finally, remember that the best way to handle a disappointed customer is to keep him from becoming one in the first place. Take preventive steps to keep problems from occurring. And if a problem does occur and you can correct it without inconveniencing the customer, do it.

SUMMING UP PART TWO. TO MANAGE ANY MOMENT OF TRUTH, ASK THE WINNING QUESTION

As I mentioned at the start of Part Two, there is no way that I can cover every possible moment of truth for every situation. However, I can give you a simple question whose answers will help you to make the best of any moment of truth, in any situation, with any customer, and at any time. Here's what I want you to do: Before and during your contact with every customer, cultivate the habit of mentally asking yourself the winning question:

How can I make him glad he talked to me?

Then start generating some answers to the question and put them to work. Some possible answers might be:

- I can help him solve a problem.
- I can save him time.
- I can save or make him money.
- I can empathize and listen to him.
- I can reassure him that we will never let him down.
- I can pay him a sincere compliment or tell him something that will make him feel better about himself.
- I can tell him an amusing experience or a funny story to brighten his day.
- I can give him something extra or add some special touch that lets him know that he's getting more than his money's worth.
- I can always let him know that I appreciate his business and ask for his advice on how I can better serve him.
- I can strive to look, sound, and act like the kind of person

that he is proud to associate with and wants to do business with.

Those are just a few of many possible answers to the winning question. I call it the winning question because putting the answers to work makes the moment of truth a winning one for both you and the customer.

And here's a final suggestion for managing every moment of truth. As you walk away from each customer:

- Visualize him with a plus sign stamped on his forehead if you think he feels rewarded. He will probably buy, multiply, and come back.
- Visualize him with a minus sign stamped on his forehead if you think he feels disappointed. He probably won't be back and will tell up to twenty people.
- Visualize him with a zero stamped on his forehead if you think he feels neutral about the experience. He may or may not come back.

That's what they train waiters and waitresses to do at TGI Friday's. It may seem like a simplistic, commonsense way to teach employees to treat customers well but there's no arguing with success. Without advertising, Friday's has achieved the highest per-unit sales volume of any restaurant chain in the nation. Word of mouth is powerful stuff.

Part Three
THE TRIPLE-WIN REWARD SYSTEM

Introduction

Motivate them, train them, care about them
and make winners out of them . . . we know that
if we treat our employees correctly, they'll treat
the customers right. And if customers are
treated right, they'll come back.

—J. W. MARRIOTT, JR.,
chairman and president, Marriott Corporation

It's great to talk about how important customers are and how it's everybody's job to do whatever it takes to win and keep them. But unless management rewards employees for providing outstanding service, you may as well forget it. It simply isn't going to happen. Employees, like customers, do things for their own reasons, not ours.

If you are an owner or manager, or someday hope to be one, this final section is about your piece of the quality service puzzle. First, we are going to review a simple, obvious principle that explains why employees behave the way they do and its implications for customer service. Then we will consider some answers to four crucial questions that every manager needs to answer in order to get everyone focusing on the customer. Finally, we will look at an action plan for creating a customer-driven, turned-on company.

20

WHAT GETS REWARDED GETS DONE

If the frontline people do count, you couldn't prove
it by examining the reward systems in most
organizations.

—KARL ALBRECHT AND RON ZEMKE

A man went fishing one day. He looked over the side of his boat and
saw a snake with a frog in its mouth. Feeling sorry for the frog, he
reached down, gently took the frog from the snake, and set the frog
free. But then he felt sorry for the snake. He looked around the
boat, but he had no food. All he had was a bottle of bourbon. So he
opened the bottle and gave the snake a few shots. The snake went
off happy, the frog was happy, and the man was happy to have
performed such good deeds. He thought everything was great until
about ten minutes passed and he heard something knock against the
side of the boat. With stunned disbelief, the fisherman looked down
and saw the snake was back with *two frogs!*

If you read my earlier book, *The Greatest Management Principle
in the World,* also known as *GMP,* * you probably recognize that
fable. Just as the story of the farmer and his three pigs illustrates the
Greatest Business Secret in the World, the story of the fisherman,
the snake, and the frog illustrate the Greatest Management Principle by giving us two important lessons.

* *GMP: The Greatest Management Principle in the World* is published in paperback
by Berkley Books, New York, in audiocassette form by Nightingale-Conant Corporation, Chicago, Illinois, and in videocassette by Coronet/MTI Film & Video, Deer-
field, Illinois.

1. You get more of the behavior that you reward. You don't get what you hope for, ask for, wish for, or beg for. You get what you reward. Come what may, all living beings are going to act in their own best interest and it's unrealistic to expect them to do otherwise.

2. In trying to do the right thing, it's oh so easy to fall into the trap of inadvertently rewarding the wrong behavior and getting the wrong results.

Like the Greatest Business Secret, the Greatest Management Principle is simple and obvious:

The Things That Get Rewarded Get Done

By and large, people behave the way the reward system teaches them to behave. And it's true for the executive, the salesperson, the typist, the janitor, or anyone else.

You would think that such a simple, obvious principle would be well recognized in most organizations. Guess again! The single greatest obstacle to effective performance in most organizations is the giant mismatch between the behavior needed and the behavior rewarded. Organizations of all kinds fall into the trap of hoping for *A*, rewarding *B*, and wondering why they get *B*. Here are a few examples:

- Corporate boards of directors ask their top-level executives to focus on long-term results, but pay them huge bonuses based on short-term profits and threaten their jobs when profits decline. Then they wonder why executives are preoccupied with short-term profits instead of long-term growth.
- University administrators ask college professors to be dedicated teachers, but the raises, promotions, and tenure go to those who do the most research and publishing. Then they wonder why students (who happen to be the customers) aren't getting the quality of education that they need.
- As voters, we ask congressmen in Washington to reduce the federal deficit, but reelect those who spend the most money on our particular special interests. Then we curse the national debt and wonder why Congress just can't seem to get it under control.

Whenever you have difficulty understanding why people behave the way that they do, all you have to do is ask the magic question:

What's Being Rewarded?

Whether it's planned or not, every organization has some kind of reward system. And sooner or later, almost everyone figures it out and behaves the way the system teaches them to behave. Reward the right behavior and you get the right results. Fail to reward the right behavior and you're going to get the wrong results. That's the simple, basic message of GMP.

The Three Key Players in the Triple Win

Whenever you see an organization consistently providing excellent service, you can be sure that there is a whole lot more than luck involved. Companies that give good service have a well-planned reward system that meets the needs and wants of three distinct parties. First, the customer must be rewarded with superior products or services, because without customers there is no business. Second, employees must be rewarded (for rewarding the customer) with adequate pay, opportunities for growth, and an environment that makes them feel like winners. Finally, the company needs to be rewarded with a meaningful profit so it can continue to grow and reward its customers, owners, and employees. The key is balance. If any one of these three groups isn't rewarded for an extended period, the quality of service and the future of the business are in jeopardy.

Picture the three components of the triple win (customers, employees, and company) as links in a chain, with employees in the middle. We have all heard the old cliché about a chain being no stronger than its weakest link, and this applies to the problem of delivering quality service to the customer. Most owners and managers fully realize that their ultimate success or failure will be determined by the customer and understand the importance of rewarding him. And they also realize that unless a reasonable profit is made, there is no point in being in business.

But the ignored link in the chain is the employee reward system. Most businesses reward employees on some basis other than taking care of the customer. And that's one key reason why customers get poor service. The typical business hires employees and managers, expects them to serve the customer, and then rewards them for something else. And something else is usually what they get. For example, here is a little quiz for you. Answer yes or no to the following ten questions and count the number of yes answers.

Does your company talk about the importance of customer service and then:

- Pay the front-line people who deal with customers a low, flat, hourly wage?
- Offer front-line people little or no training in the fundamentals of providing quality service or managing the moments of truth?
- Offer front-line employees no extra incentives for taking special care of the customer?
- Reprimand or punish employees when service is poor but take it for granted when service is great?
- Place a much greater emphasis on winning new customers than on helping and serving the ones it already has?
- Offer no rewards or recognition to non–customer-contact employees for their efforts in serving the customer?
- Frequently hold "Be nice to the customer" rallies or campaigns that last for a specified period and are soon forgotten?
- Have top managers who rarely, if ever, devote their time and energy to listening to customers and helping them solve their problems?
- Make no effort measure the level of service quality as perceived by the customer?
- Make no attempt to hold managers at all levels accountable or reward them on the basis of the quality of service provided?

Unless you work for one of the few companies that provide outstanding service, you probably answered yes to most of those questions. Most businesses put people in front-line positions, pay them a low, flat wage, give them little or no training, and expect them to give excellent service. To make bad matters worse, the word "customer" is rarely, if ever, heard by employees who don't deal directly with them. And as for managers, practically none (with the exception of sales managers) are rewarded by any criteria that are remotely related to serving the customer. Then, when the customer complaints start rolling in and revenues decline, these same owners and managers wring their hands in frustration and tell themselves, "You just can't find good help anymore." It's another example of the folly of hoping for *A* and rewarding *B*.

Through the Looking Glass

There are three basic ways for a manager to teach employees how to treat customers:

- Tell them what you want.
- Show them what you want.
- Measure and reward what you want.

Where service is excellent, the people in charge do a whole lot more than tell employees what they want. They act as role models and show a genuine concern for customers by taking the time to listen to and help them. And they back up their commitment to customer service by looking for, measuring, recognizing, and rewarding performance that results in good service at all levels and in all jobs. On the other hand, where service is poor, management talks about how important customers are but is just too busy to deal directly with them, And employees are rewarded for showing up, looking busy, company politics, administrivia, or something other than rewarding the customer. In other words, *how customers get treated is a direct reflection of how management is treating employees.*

When service is poor, it's all too common to see the blame laid at the feet of unions, the government, lazy workers, or other scapegoats. But it's also a huge mistake. Through its own behavior and the reward system, management is telling employees that customers just aren't very important. And that speaks louder than all the verbal messages in the world. Employees may listen to what you say, but they will believe what you do. And they will do what you measure and reward. It's not a sure-fire, guaranteed formula but it's the way to bet. More than 80 percent of all behavior is determined by the reward system.

What's being rewarded where you work? Is it taking care of the customer or something else? But a much more important question is, *What needs to be rewarded to create a customer-driven team where you work and how should you go about it?* Read the final two chapters and you'll find out.

21

HOW TO KEEP THE SPOTLIGHT ON THE CUSTOMER

A service performance measurement system will get employees' attention. A well-executed reward system will keep it. Service providers realize that management is serious about quality when management is willing to pay for it.

—A. PARASURAMAN, VALARIE A. ZEITHAML,
AND LEONARD L. BERRY

Customer: May I have a glass of water, please?
Waiter: Sorry, that's not my table.

Citizen: Am I in the right line to get a license plate?
Government employee holding an opened can of beans: I'm at lunch.

Passenger: Where is Gate 23B?
Flight attendant: Ask someone else. I'm off duty.

Patient: Why doesn't someone answer the telephone?
Clinic employee: It ain't my phone.

Ignored customer: Does anybody work here?
Auto dealership mechanic: What's wrong with you?

You don't have to be a customer very long to find out that such moments of truth are too common. All five of the above happened to me in the same year. No business will ever be totally immune to such embarrassments. But when they occur with regularity, you can be sure that the reward system is not customer-driven.

Getting an employee, group, or organization of any size to focus on rewarding the customer takes two main ingredients. First, it takes a reward system that rewards employees for rewarding the customer. Second, it takes leaders who set the tone with their own customer-driven behavior. The success of such a strategy depends on every manager finding the right answers to four key questions. Let's look at those questions and consider some answers that will help keep your team thinking and acting with the customer's best interest in mind. The first question that you need to answer is:

What Kind of Behavior and Results Do I Want?

Good management always starts with clearly communicated expectations and solid, *specific*, written goals. Begin by asking every employee and work group to write an answer to the following question in 250 words (one page) or less:

What results do I (we) produce and how do they benefit the customer?

Answering this question will force everyone to think about the basics of their job in terms of the customer. Everyone, not just front-line employees, needs to answer the question. For example, a janitor's answer might be, "I keep the place clean and orderly so that customers will enjoy visiting here and other employees can do a better job of serving the customer." Or a production planner might answer, "I coordinate and schedule production runs that make it possible for our customers to get the right goods, at the right place, and at the right time."

Then sit down with each person (or group if it's a group goal) and decide what results he is to attain by a certain date. Here are some guidelines that will help you assist people in setting good goals:

- Their goals should contribute to helping you achieve your goals and the company's ultimate goal of serving the customer.
- State the goal in terms of the results you want to achieve and not the activities you perform. For example, being nice to customers is a nebulous activity. Reducing the number of customer complaints by 30 percent is a result.

- Goals should be brief, simple, and written to increase clarity and commitment. And keep the number of goals small. More than two or three goals end up becoming no goals.
- Let people set their own goals whenever you can. It increases motivation and commitment. If someone prefers that you set a goal for him, do it. What matters most is that you both understand the results he is trying to achieve.
- Challenging but attainable goals get the best performance. Encourage people to choose battles big enough to matter but small enough to win.

Once you and your team have decided on which goals to pursue, you are ready to tackle the second question:

How Will I Measure It?

Many years ago, W. C. Fields was napping in his dressing room when a stage manager stuck his head in the door and cried, "You're on!" Waking from his slumber, Fields sat up in a stupor and replied, "How am I doing?" That's one question that all employees need to know the answer to.

People do what gets measured. I cannot stress that point too strongly. Every important goal needs to be accompanied with a way to keep score so that you and your team can measure the progress toward the results you are trying to get. Additionally, keeping score and letting people know how they are doing is a tremendous motivational tool. How much do you think people would enjoy playing golf, tennis, baseball, basketball, football, video games, or Monopoly if there wasn't any way to keep score?

Almost anything can be measured in either dollars, percentages, or units in a given period. For example, some common measures are:

- Dollars of sales per month
- Number of customer complaints received per week
- Number of complimentary letters received per month
- Percentage of on-time deliveries per month
- Number of square feet cleaned per day
- Percentage of defective merchandise returned per quarter
- Percentage of sales dollars coming from repeat customers

Even nebulous concepts such as customer perceptions of relative quality can be measured with a rating scale (as pointed out in Chapter 8) and used as a basis for tracking and improving. When deciding what to use as a performance measure, keep these points in mind:

- Don't let anybody con you into believing that you can't measure what they do. If what they are doing can't be measured, they aren't contributing.
- Keep it simple. Otherwise, people will spend too much time measuring, rather than pursuing their goals.
- Measure progress toward goals achieved and not activities. For example, in golf the goal is to complete the course with the minimum number of strokes, so you count the number of strokes. You don't count how far the ball is hit, how far the golfer walks (or rides) or how much he sweats. Take a similar approach in measuring goals on the job. A good measurement system encourages smart work, not busy work.
- Remember that it's far more important to measure group goals than individual goals. Team performance counts most.

Finally, remember that the best performance measures give employees frequent feedbacks so that they can see how they are doing and adjust their behavior accordingly. In their excellent book *Service America!,* authors Karl Albrecht and Ron Zemke tell of giving a one-hour lecture on the importance of feedback as a performance-improvement tool. At the end of the hour, a participant stood and said:

> Let me see if I got all that. There are two things we have to go to get better results: first, we have to have agreed-upon measurements for each department; second we have to have a method of putting the measurements up where everybody can see 'em. That don't seem so tough.*

Whenever you have an important goal to achieve, consider putting up a scoreboard, chart, poster, or some highly visible perfor-

*Karl Albrecht and Ron Zemke, *Service America! (Homewood, Illinois, Dow Jones-Irwin, 1985), p. 142.

mance indicator. Update it frequently and put it where those responsible for achieving the goal can see it. It will keep your team focused on the right goals and tell them how they are doing. It's a simple and very effective technique for improving performance, if you then answer our third question and follow through:

How Will I Reward It When I Get It?

Goals and measures only start people moving in the right direction. You need specific rewards to keep them moving. Remember, the right rewards for the right behavior get the right results. The reason so many goal-setting programs fail is that they aren't directly linked to the reward system.

In thinking about rewards it helps to break them into three categories:

1. Conditional rewards are those that are promised and handed out for achieving specifically stated goals. Production bonuses, sales commissions, and promotions for improving service quality to an agreed-on level are all examples of conditional rewards.

2. On-the-spot rewards are the ones handed out immediately for behavior that you want to encourage. For example, as a manager, it's important for you to get out and look for the good things that your people are doing for the customer. And when you see behavior that you like, find some way to reward your employee for it immediately. Pull him to the side and praise him. Then follow up by writing him a congratulatory letter and putting it in his file. Or praise him in front of his peers at the next meeting. Some companies employ mystery shoppers whose sole purpose is to catch employees doing things right. And when they do, the employee is immediately rewarded with cash payments and praised, and the incident is written up and reported to management for special recognition.

3. Surprise rewards are rewards bestowed for achieving exceptional performance. For example, when Scandanavian Air Systems was chosen "best business class airline in the world" by its passengers, Jan Carlzon threw a very special Christmas party for all employees. Employees were transported to and from the all-you-can-eat-and-drink affair in rented limousines, and Carlzon gave every employee a gold watch. It was his way of saying "thank you" to everyone for their help in turning SAS into a profitable, high service quality airline.

The number of ways to reward good performance is limited only by your imagination. The next time you are trying to decide what to use as a reward, here are ten types of rewards to consider:

MONEY

It works great, *if you base pay on performance*. Commissions, bonuses, piece rates, and payments tied to achieving results are all very effective. In our materialistic society, money is power, prestige, and the most common yardstick of success. People who tell you that money can't buy performance just don't know where to shop.

For example, consider the case of the Mixon Tire Company of Minneapolis–Saint Paul, Minnesota. In 1985, owner Bud Mixon made the employees of his six stores the following offer: "Whenever your store goes one full week with no customer complaints, I'll pay everyone a dollar an hour more for the entire week." Each customer was given a comment card to fill in and mail back. The card asked customers to rate the quality of service and tell of any problems that they might have encountered. The comment cards and any other complaints from dissatisfied customers were used as the way to keep score. To insure that production was kept high, mechanics were offered a production bonus as well. Mixon knew that complaint-free service would generate enough repeat and referral business to more than cover the dollar-an-hour increase in wages, and it did. Complaints dropped over 75 percent, from an average of several per week at each store to only one or two per month. Some stores went as long as three weeks in a row with zero complaints.

Mixon's plan for improving service has a number of important strong points that a good customer service incentive plan should have:

- The goal is simple to understand, attainable, and easily measurable.
- The rewards are based on team performance. This creates positive peer pressure and lessens the chances of anyone loafing or saying, "That's not my job" or "I'm off duty" to a customer. How would you like to face your peers knowing that your negligence cost each of them an average of forty dollars?
- It's a continuing program and not a one-shot campaign.

Every week is a new challenge and a new chance to make the bonus.
- The responsibility for eliminating complaints is placed squarely on the shoulders of all employees.

Similarly, in a manufacturing setting, bonuses for providing quality goods to the customer can pay off handsomely. At Quanex Corporation's Fort Smith, Arkansas, steel mill, each bar of steel comes with a rare guarantee. If a buyer has to recondition a Fort Smith bar (it's common for steel buyers to have to shave, sheer, or smooth a bar, which means added cost) he gets it free. But behind the guarantee is an employee bonus plan based on the number of quality tons shipped. The more quality tons made, the greater the production bonus, which is divided equally among production crews. But when customers reject a bar, that amount is subtracted from the following month's production total. Everyone has a stake in producing superior quality and it's paying off handsomely. While most mills consider a 2 percent rejection rate as good, the rejection rate at Fort Smith is about 0.1 percent. The typical domestic steel plant takes an average of 5.8 man hours to produce and ship a ton of steel. At Fort Smith it takes 2.5 man hours and the plant is making a healthy profit in a supposedly dying industry.

RECOGNITION AND PRAISE

A reward system that bases pay on performance will get and keep almost everyone's attention. But if you don't have the authority or the budget to reward with dollars, consider rewarding with recognition. It usually costs little or nothing and it's the most powerful reward of all. People want to feel important and appreciated more than anything else, and a well-planned recognition program will get you incredible dedication. Employee-of-the-month awards with the employee's picture on the wall, changes in title, certificates, citations, trophies, plaques, personal congratulatory letters from top management, honors or awards presented at banquets, special pins or other jewelry, favorable publicity, and anything that connotes status make excellent recognition rewards.

In 1986, I checked into the Sheraton Saint Louis Hotel in downtown Saint Louis. In my registration packet was a booklet of coupons. Printed on the cover was a message that read as follows:

As our customer, you are very important. Would you mind taking this praising coupon book? When you see any of our hotel staff doing something right or treating you well, would you get their name and present them with a praising coupon or turn it in to the front desk?

"What a stroke of genius!" I thought to myself. Here is a hotel that's going to build an outstanding service reputation by letting the customers tell them who's doing something right and rewarding and recognizing the deserving employees. And that's exactly what the Sheraton Saint Louis is doing.

The so-called "praising coupons" are the brainchild of the Sheraton Saint Louis Quality Committee. Employees redeem coupons for points that can be turned into cash prizes, Sheraton T-shirts, coffee mugs, clock radios, sports tickets, and other symbols of recognition for outstanding service. The idea has worked so well that the hotel started using "back-of-the-house praising coupons." Whenever a front-line employee, such as a waiter, gets outstanding help from a non–front-line employee, such as a cook, the waiter gives the cook a coupon for helping him serve the customer. As Ron Tarson, head of training and development at the hotel, puts it, "When I see an employee having a good week, I'll tell him, 'You're having a good week. You got two coupons.' Just the attention from management makes all the difference. A lot more people are willing to take a chance to be outstanding."

An old saying from the military has it that a man won't sell you his life for a million dollars, but he will gladly give it to you for a piece of ribbon. Whether you chose to use pins, mugs, T-shirts, congratulatory letters, applause, or whatever, remember that praise and public recognition for outstanding service are the most powerful rewards at your disposal.

Money and recognition are the two most powerful rewards. Almost everyone responds to praises and raises. And it's best to award some money with recognition. If you keep praising and recognizing people without paying them, pretty soon they start thinking, "If we are so great, why don't they pay us more?"

EIGHT OTHER WAYS TO REWARD GREAT SERVICE

Money and recognition aren't the only ways to reward good service. Briefly, here are eight more:

Time off. Give people an afternoon, a day, or more off for achieving an agreed-on goal or doing something extra special for a customer.

At Marshall Field and Company, every time a store manager observes a salesperson being extra helpful to a customer, he gives the employee a silver coin called a "Frangloon." Ten coins are worth a box of Field's Frango mint chocolates and 100 earn an extra day of paid vacation. Four years ago it took a Marshall Field's salesperson an average of 10 minutes to approach a customer. But thanks to computer-aided scheduling that puts salespersons where they are neded most and the incentive plan, the average approach time has been reduced from 10 to 2 minutes.

A piece of the action. Workers who get rewarded like owners behave like owners. Give them part ownership or a percentage of the profits as part of their pay. That will definitely get them thinking about the customer.

Favorite work. Give people more of the work they enjoy most as a reward and excuse them from work that they least enjoy. Since people usually like to do what they do best, this is a great way to get more excellent work from your best performers.

Advancement. Promotions and increased responsibilities are the most common types of advancement rewards. It's hard to keep your best people if they don't feel that they are progressing in their careers.

Freedom. In jobs that have been tightly controlled with time clocks and rigid working hours, freedom and autonomy can be excellent rewards. In essence you tell people, "Do a good job and you can be your own boss." Let them set their own hours or do part of the job at home as a freedom reward. As one young worker put it, "I don't mind being pushed as long as I can steer."

Personal growth. Challenging new assignments that cause people to stretch their abilities, the chance to acquire new skills, and educational opportunities can all be used as personal growth rewards. This is an important reward for professional and technical employees.

Prizes. Vacations, raffles, free dinners, gift certificates, sports or theater tickets, and company products and services are examples of using prizes as performance incentives.

In its famous Thanks a Million contest, The Southland Corporation, parent of 7-Eleven Stores, allowed seventeen employees and franchises, judged to have performed outstanding feats of customer service, to participate in a sweepstakes with one million dollars to be awarded to the winner. On Friday, February 13, 1987, Debra Wilson, a Plano, Texas, 7-Eleven store manager and divorced mother of two, won fifty thousand dollars a year for the next twenty years. Now you understand why the company slogan is, "Oh, thank Heaven for 7-Eleven."

Fun. A good manager works at building fun into the workplace and uses it as an incentive to build morale, participation, and involvement. Parties to celebrate special birthdays, anniversaries, or special achievements, bulletin boards for jokes, photographs and stories, piped-in music, and company sports teams are all examples of ways for people to have fun on the job and boost morale. If your workplace is too busy for people to laugh and have fun occasionally, then it's just too busy.

No matter what incentives you use to make work fun, *make your team feel like winners!* People love to identify with groups that give them a feeling of success and will do almost anything for the privilege. If you doubt that, look at the money that changes hands every day as people gladly pay their hard-earned dollars to identify with winning sports teams. Work at building that type of pride on the job. It's a tremendous motivator and energy builder.

Once you have decided the results and behavior you want, how to measure them, and how to reward them, you need to find some answers to one more crucial question:

How Can I Show Employees That the Customer Comes First?

Norman Vincent Peale once remarked, "Nothing is more confusing than people who give good advice but set bad examples." For a manager it's important to lead with rewards, but it isn't enough. You also have to lead with your actions. And that means getting out from behind your desk, meeting and talking to customers about their wants, and finding out from your employees how you can help them help the customer. Customer-driven managers talk about, reward, and live the message that rewarding the customer is the name of the game.

For example, J. W. "Bill" Marriott, Marriott Corporation's chairman and president, logs over two hundred thousand miles each year in the air visiting the various hotels and other properties and setting the tone for the rest of the organization. As Marriott puts it, "If I sit back and relax, a lot of other people will sit back and relax. After all, if you're going to be a star performer, you can't sit back and relax. A star performer has to work hard and make sacrifices, and at Marriott Corporation, we do both."

Similarly, the Dallas-based Southland Corporation demonstrates its commitment to customer service by having managers lead by example. Each of Southland's three thousand managers is required to get out of his office, put on a smock, and work at least one eight-hour shift per year in a 7-Eleven Store, to keep him in touch with customers. As you might expect, one of the very first managers to work a shift at a 7-Eleven was Southland's president, Jere W. Thompson.

Another important facet of Southland's commitment to service is the Neighborhood Walk program. In this program, store managers and franchisees walk through the neighborhood of the nearby 7-Eleven and knock on doors. They introduce themselves to residents and give them a gift packet containing coupons redeemable for free beverages at the store, a personal letter from the store manager, and a comment card that the customer can mail in later. The purpose of the program is to personalize the service, get customer feedback, and put a face behind the 7-Eleven name.

In summary, putting and keeping the spotlight on the customer begins with every manager finding the answer to four crucial questions:

- What behavior and results do I want?
- How will I measure it?
- How will I reward it when I get it?
- How can I show employees that the customer comes first?

Once you have the right answers, you're ready for action. And action is what the final chapter is all about.

22

THE QUALITY CUSTOMER SERVICE ACTION PLAN

Success is turning knowledge into positive action.

—DOROTHY LEEDS

A man went to a doctor feeling run-down and fatigued. After a thorough diagnosis and examination the doctor told him, "The best thing for you to do is to give up smoking, give up drinking, get up at sunrise, and go to bed early at night." After a moment of silent reflection, the patient shook his head and said, "Doc, I really don't deserve the best. What's second best?"

When it comes to providing excellent service, a lot of today's business owners and managers remind me of that patient. They realize that their service quality is ailing and is in serious need of improvement. But instead of making a serious commitment to improving it, they opt for Band-Aid solutions. The troops are given a rousing speech about the importance of service and April is declared "Be nice to the customer month." The walls are plastered with empty slogans and front-line employees are sent to smile training classes. And not surprisingly, the employees take it with a grain of salt and think to themselves, "This, too, shall pass."

If you are an owner or top manager, I have a very important question for you about the quality of your service:

Do You Want to Act or Do You Want to Talk?

There is no deep, dark secret to providing quality customer service. It all begins with the behavior of management, starting at the very top. The few organizations that provide great service do so because the top brass puts their time, effort, and money where their mouth is. They make service a continuing, company-wide top priority. They provide extensive training to their front-line people on the basics of excellent service and managing the moments of truth. They personally involve themselves in the business of listening to and helping both employees and customers. Then they set service goals, measure the quality of service, and reward employees for delivering. It's a heavy, long-range investment of time and money that more than pays for itself. In short, they continually practice what I call the service management cycle:

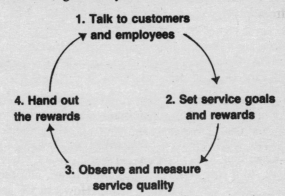

1. Talk to customers and employees

2. Set service goals and rewards

3. Observe and measure service quality

4. Hand out the rewards

The companies that don't provide great service would like to but they just aren't willing to pay the price. They talk about how important customers are but provide little or no service training and make no effort to measure the quality of service or reward employees accordingly. In short, their commitment to service is lip service. It sort of reminds me of the bum who said, "I'd give a hundred dollars to be one of them millionaires."

If you aren't willing to pay the price to deliver quality service, then don't mention it to your employees or customers. It's a waste of everyone's time and will get you a poor service image as a company that delivers less than it promises. If you are going to be mediocre, just keep quiet, offer bargain-basement prices, and pray that your competitors are no better than you.

But if you are serious about providing excellent service, this final chapter is your blueprint for action. Building on much of what you have learned thus far, the following action plan contains the basic ingredients for making a customer-driven team out of any size organization. The plan consists of seven major recommendations.

1. Treat Your Customers Like Lifetime Partners

How would you treat a customer if you knew that:

- You were going to see him every workday for the rest of your life.
- He would visit you at work every day.
- At the end of each visit, he would decide to buy something from either you or one of your competitors.

Chances are you would treat this customer extremely well, because he has the potential to be a real gold mine or a tremendous waste of time. For example, you would make an extra effort to listen to him carefully and find out what his wants and needs were. You would focus on helping him buy what was right for him, rather than fast-talking him into buying what you had in stock. You would do whatever was possible to make sure that you didn't disappoint him or make him angry, because he would make a buying decision every day. And you would certainly want to ask him the platinum questions, "How are we doing?" and "How can we get better?" Well, that's precisely how you should strive to treat every customer. Even if your product or service is one that people buy only once in a lifetime, the effort will pay off handsomely with referrals. Great service makes for great word-of-mouth advertising.

One key to getting people to behave the way you want is to treat them the way you want them to become. For better or worse, we all tend to live up to others' expectations of us. So, if you want to keep customers for life, start treating them like lifetime partners. Think of them as an integral part of your business, just like managers, salespersons, and secretaries.

Why not make a place for them on your organization chart?

Chances are you have never seen an organization chart with a box labeled "customers" on it. Most charts have places for stockholders, board members, and presidents. Some have designations for line and staff positions. Still others have elaborate symbols to indicate who in the organization has what kind of authority and how much. Yet the one group of people with final authority is invariably left off the chart. Could this be one reason that the customer so often gets forgotten?

If your business has an organization chart, make a new box at the very top and label it "customers." This will communicate to everyone who the real boss in your business is. In the final analysis, it's the customer who makes the final decisions on whether or not you stay in business and how much money you make. I don't know any owner, manager, or employee who can afford to ignore a boss with that kind of clout. Do you?

Putting customers on your chart acknowledges them as a part of your team, but it's only a symbolic gesture. Here are four other strategies for treating customers like lifetime partners with some accompanying questions to ponder.

Know your customers and their buying motives. Do you have a clear picture of what specific kinds of customers you want to win and keep? What good feelings and solutions to problems are they looking for? Whether you base your analysis on age, sex, educational level, income level, region, or whatever, the more clearly you can define who your customers are, the greater are the chances of winning and keeping them. Conversely, if you try to be all things to all people, you'll end up being nobody to everybody.

Be easy to do business with. Are your employees and systems friendly and easily accessible? Do you have an 800 number customers can call to resolve their problems, place an order, or get information quickly? Have you taken the risk out of the buying decision with a money-back guarantee? When the customer gets your bill, is the return envelope postpaid or is it inscribed with a terse note ordering him to put a stamp on it?

Make your customers aware of the great service you give. What are you doing to build value and pleasantly surprise the customer? Are you using customer complaints as an opportunity to build and increase customer loyalty? How do you stay in touch with the customer and help him get better use of your products or services? What are you doing, in a subtle way, to make him aware of the great service you are giving him? Remember, when it comes to service quality, the customer's perception is everything.

Get frequent feedback. Are you making the effort to look at your business through your customer's eyes? Are you regularly asking the golden and platinum questions? Do you have a systematic approach to measuring and tracking customer perceptions of service quality? And most important, what are you doing with the information that you get from the customer? Are you using it as a basis for improving service or is it being filed and forgotten?

No, you're never going to make every customer, or maybe any customer, a lifetime partner. But that's not the point. The point is that by striving to treat them this way you'll have them buying, multiplying, and coming back in large numbers simply because your service is so great.

2. Ask Everyone Where You Work for Service Improvement Ideas

Here's a good rule of thumb: When it comes to service quality, customers know the score but employees know how it got that way. Ask customers to tell you what your level of service quality is and what to work on to improve it. Then ask employees why your level of service quality is what it is and how to go about improving it.

To carry the sports analogy one step further, the customer is the scorekeeper, but the employees are the players and coaches that can tell you why things are going the way they are and how to make them better. While you need to know what the score is, you also need to know why it got that way and how to go about improving it. And employees are your best source for this type of information. The person who does the job every day usually has the best insight about why things do or don't work and the best ideas for making improvements. Simply asking employees for their ideas provides a tremendous, but often overlooked, reservoir of knowledge and creativity. Why not tap it?

Ask everyone who works in your organization to answer these two questions:

- What's the biggest, most frequently occurring problem that you face in trying to serve the customer?

- If you were the president and could make only one change to improve the quality of customer service, what would you do?

Make it a contest, complete with rewards and recognition for those persons or groups with the best answers. If an idea makes or saves money, consider giving a piece of the profits to the creator. And most important, when you get a good idea, put it to work and let it be known that it's an employee-generated idea. People like to be proud of what they do and will support what they help create. Once employees see that you are serious about putting their ideas to work, you'll get plenty of them.

3. If You Don't Have a Service Strategy, Get One

"Federal Express, when it absolutely positively has to be there overnight."

"At Ford, quality is Job One."

"Hallmark, when you care enough to send the very best."

"Like a good neighbor, State Farm is there."

Those are four slogans that you are probably familiar with. Each is a short message that tells both customers and employees what the essence of the company's service is, why it is different from the competition, and why it is worth buying from. Such is the nature of a well-thought-out service strategy, and if your company doesn't have one, get one.

Your service strategy doesn't have to be poetic but it should be brief and communicated over and over and over to your employees. For example, "Within the Disney organization, quality service means an unending devotion to creating pleasurable experiences for people," according to Ben Chester, director of corporate communications. And according to Harry Mullikin, chairman and CEO of Westin Hotels and Resorts, quality customer service means "Caring, comfortable and civilized—it is our intention at Westin Hotels and Resorts that you will always find us that way."

The essence of leadership is the ability to articulate a vision and get people to follow it. And providing and delivering service is no exception to the rule. Your employees and customers need a clear picture of what service you are in the business of providing and why you are different from the competition. If you don't have a service strategy, work on defining, developing, and polishing one. Get to the point where everyone in the company can recite verbatim, in a sentence or two, precisely what your company does for the customer and why it is unique. And one final word of caution: Put a lot of time and thought into formulating your strategy, and once you have it, stick with it. Empty new slogans that appear every month or so will just be ignored or laughed at by all concerned. Decide what your company stands for, say it, stick with it, and back it up with performance.

4. Carefully Select and Heavily Train Your Front-Line People in the Art of Quality Customer Service

Excellent service on the part of front-line employees is usually the result of a process of careful selection, plenty of customer service training, and a well-designed reward system. Screen your front-line job applicants for people skills. Have they worked with customers before? If so, verify their social skills with their former employer. In the interview process, give them a customer service problem that they would be likely to encounter on the job (such as an angry or a complaining customer) and ask them, "What would you do?" A number of psychological tests are available for assessing interpersonal skills and you may want to consider using one or more of them. Quality employees are a crucial ingredient for quality service.

It's all too common to find front-line positions filled by rude, obnoxious people whose only proficiency seems to be a knack for running off customers. If you have such organizational kamikazes where you work, either get rid of them or put them in a job where they don't deal directly with customers. If they have talents that can be used elsewhere in the company, that's great. Otherwise, tell them "Sayonara." Leaving them on the front line is economic suicide and unfair to the rest of your employees, who are working hard to please the customer. But a word of caution: If you find a number of employees being rude to customers, the problem may be contact overload. The best of employees burn out with too much exposure to too many customers.

As for training, the best customer service training is thorough and a continuing part of every employee's job. Shallow, one-shot programs that tell employees to smile and give the customer a "warm fuzzy" may amuse and entertain employees for a day, but aren't likely to produce much residual benefit. If your front-line people have to be trained to be nice, they probably don't have the social aptitude to be on the front line in the first place.

While it's important to stress being nice to customers, good training gives front-line employees a whole lot more than that. A good initial program will give new or untrained employees:

- Specific information on your company's service goals
- Information that they need about your company's products and services
- A basic understanding of what it takes to win and keep customers
- Problem-solving ideas and techniques for identifying and managing the moments of truth in their jobs

Furthermore, for training to be effective, it has to be followed up with spaced repetition and on-the-job applications. Books, workbooks, newsletters, payroll inserts, guest speakers, audiocassettes, and videocassettes are all valuable aids for hammering home the quality service message.

One of the best ways to make service training effective is to combine it with asking employees for their ideas. Why not have them meet for an hour or two each week in quality service groups? A good quality service group can serve three important functions:

- *Training.* In the groups they can learn the latest concepts of customer service, from books, cassette tapes, articles, video training, or whatever.
- *Information sharing.* Through informal discussions they can learn how to improve service from each other's on-the-job experiences. For example, if Jack learns Mary's foolproof method for finding out what the customer really wants, that's going to make Jack a better and more valuable employee.
- *Problem solving.* The group can take the ideas they learn at the sessions and apply them to solving specific service problems on the job.

Make the meetings voluntary, informal, and fun. Serve refreshments and hold them on company time. Ask each group to choose only one or two problems to work on at a time and give them the support they need to solve their problems. You may want to make it a contest and give a nice prize or reward to the group whose idea has the most positive impact on customer service. Remember, the people closest to the job usually have the best ideas for improving it. And the practical application of classroom learning is the best way to reinforce training.

Finally, no matter what type of front-line training format you use, ask your employees to identify as many of their moments of truth with customers as they can. Then, for each moment of truth, have them answer the following three questions:

- What good feeling or solutions to problems does the customer want at that moment?
- What's his emotional state? Is he glad, mad, scared, or sad?
- How can we do a better job of making him glad he talked to us and helping him solve his problems?

Then have them answer two more questions:

- How will we know if we are getting better at managing the moments of truth? (In other words, what are we going to use to measure our progress? Customer surveys? Number of complaints? Number of compliments?)
- When we get better, how should we be rewarded for it?

All of which leads to our fifth recommendation.

5. Set Service Quality Goals and Rewards

Asking employees for their service improvement ideas will get them involved, but it takes more than involvement to improve service. It takes commitment, and there is a big difference between involvement and commitment. The kamikaze pilot who flew a hundred missions may have been involved, but he certainly wasn't committed.

The best way of enlisting a commitment to service quality is through a system that holds every work group and every manager accountable for achieving measurable, service-oriented goals and hands out rewards based on performance. Everyone, from the president on down, needs to be rewarded on the basis of some measurable contribution to service quality. Setting service-oriented goals just for front-line employees and their managers isn't enough. The commitment and accountability has to start at the top and permeate the entire organization. Rewarding top managers with big bonuses for short-term profits isn't going to get a long-term commitment to customer service. But an executive bonus that's partly based on customer perception of service quality will start the ball rolling in the right direction.

Using the guidelines in Chapter 21, establish service goals and rewards for every manager and work group for a specified period. The process should start at the top and filter down. For example, if you are the president, formulate your goals first. Then, share them with your vice-presidents and ask them to set goals that will contribute to the achievement of your goals. When the process is completed, everyone in the organization should know what his service goal is, how it's measured, the deadline for achieving it, and how he will be rewarded for achieving it. The basic idea is to create a reward system in which your employees get what they want, you get what you want, and the customer gets good service.

Once goals have been defined, sit down and write a goals-rewards contract with each person or group. The contract should be no more than one page and should specifically state what goal each is responsible for achieving, by when, and how each will be rewarded for achieving it. Then both the manager and the achievers should sign the document and each keep a copy.

You may be asking, How do I decide to reward each person? The best way is to ask them. Some people prefer money, others want time off, and still othes like prizes. If you can, let them choose among rewards of roughly equal value. One way to do this is to set up a system under which employees earn points that can be redeemed for money, prizes, time off, or whatever each employee wants. That's usually more effective than giving everyone the same kind of reward.

Also, it's generally a good idea to avoid setting all-or-nothing rewards. Set up a scale or a rate of rewards (much like a sales commission) so that the better the performance, the greater the rewards. All-or-nothing rewards can work well in a short-term situation (no customer complaints for the week earns a bonus) or when given as an additional reward for outstanding performance (sell a million dollars worth of product and you win an all-expense-paid vacation for you and your spouse).

In most, but not all cases, it's best to give rewards based on team performance. For example, Bud Mixon gave each tire store employee a cash bonus every week the store had no customer complaints. If you reward people on the basis of their individual effort, they will give you great individual effort. But if you reward them on the basis of what the group does, you'll get teamwork. In short, if you want stars, reward your stars. But if you want team players, reward teamwork.

At the end of the period, take out the goals-rewards contract, review it, and give out the rewards on the basis of what the contract stipulates. At the same time, set new goals for the next period and review what went right, what went wrong, and why. Are the goals correct? Is the level of achievement set too high or too low? Does the measurement accurately reflect what you are trying to achieve? Are the rewards fair? This is the time to decide how to do even better next time.

When things go poorly, don't point fingers at anyone or allow others to do the same. This is a problem-solving and not a blame-placing process. Point out to people what they did well and give them plenty of praise for their effort. When you have to be critical, praise the worker, criticize the work. And the subject of praise has a lot to do with the next recommendation.

6. Get Out of Your Office and Find Out What's Happening

The best managers and leaders realized long ago that you can't lead or make decisions in a vacuum. Sitting in an office reading memos and reports about what's going on in the real world is a poor substitute for seeing it firsthand. You need to actually get out and see the behavior of both customers and employees. Watch your customers and employees interacting. Be a role model and take your turn on the front line waiting on the customer for a day, as the Southland Corporation managers are doing. Ask customers the golden and platinum questions and ask employees what you can do to help them do their jobs better. Remember, your own behavior tells employees just how important you believe customers are.

Another important reason to get out of your office is to catch your employees giving great service. And when you catch them, hand out on-the-spot rewards. Too many managers today practice what Ken Blanchard calls "Seagull Management." You never hear from seagull managers when things go right. But when things go wrong, they fly in, dump on the employees and fly off. I'm sure that practically all of us have worked for a seagull or two in our careers.

Make it a habit to regularly look for employees who are doing something special for the customer. Imagine them wearing a sign that says, "Catch me being good." And when you catch them, find some way to reward them and chances are that the behavior will be repeated. One of the best rewards that every manager can use is praise. A pat on the back doesn't cost a dime and it works beautifully. To have the greatest effect, your message should contain the following ingredients:

- Make it specific.
- Make it honest. Superficial flattery and gladhanding won't work.
- Personalize it.
- Do it as soon as you see the behavior. Praise, like champagne, should be served while it's still bubbling.
- Make it proportionate to the importance of what the employee did.
- Be concrete. Don't say "nice job" or "good work." Instead, say something like, "Bill, you really know how to make customers feel appreciated. That's the fourth time I've seen you turn an angry customer into a loyal patron. I'm going to make a note of this and put it in your file. It's people like you who keep us in the black and I want you to know how much we appreciate your efforts."

Of course, if you can give Bill a cash payment, a free dinner, or some other reward in addition to praising him, that's even better and will reinforce his behavior that much more. But the point is that you can always give praise and it almost always works.

If you see an employee behaving improperly, pull him aside immediately. Let him know in no uncertain terms that the customers pay everyone's salary and that you can't afford to lose them. Point out both the correct and incorrect parts of his behavior. Then ask him, "How will you handle a similar situation next time?" If he thinks through the problem and comes up with his own solution, chances are better that he will remember and practice it than if you tell him what to do. Work with him until he has a clear understanding of how to react when confronted with a similar moment of truth. Then close by telling him something like, "I know you'll do better next time. Let me know if I can help you or if you have any questions. Remember, to the customer, you are the company."

7. Always Be Patient but Never Be Satisfied

A popular story has it that an old bull and his young son were out grazing one day on a mountainside. When they reached the mountaintop, they looked down into the valley on the other side and saw a herd of nothing but cows. Not a single bull was in sight. With youthful exuberance, the young bull shouted, "Daddy, Daddy, look at all those cows down there! Let's run down there and get us one!" After a moment of thoughtful reflection, the old bull replied, "No, Son. Let's walk down and get 'em all."

As you work to improve your level of service quality, take the old bull's approach. Take your time, be patient, and always try to get 'em all, realizing full well that you probably never will. Service quality isn't one long race. It's millions of short races one after another. Every day there will be numerous moments of truth and each one is a new chance to make it a plus for the customer. When things go wrong, learn from it and realize that even the best companies have negative, embarrassing moments every day. The key is to continually try to get better. Progress is never the work of contented people. To become smug or complacent about your level of service quality is tantamount to rolling out the red carpet for the Success Syndrome. (If you forgot the Success Syndrome, it's in Chapter 1.) Today's contented companies, managers, and employees are tomorrow's has-beens.

According to Willa A. Foster, "Quality is never an accident; it is always the result of high intention, sincere effort, intelligent direction, and skillful execution; it represents the wise choice of many alternatives." Whether you call them customers, clients, patients, subscribers, members, students, passengers, accounts, or whatever, business is pretty rotten without them. And the quality of your service will ultimately determine how many you win and keep. Good luck. Like the old bull, I hope you "get 'em all."

Epilogue

Now you know the greatest business secret in the world: *Reward the customer*. The next time you want to win customers, ask the golden question, *What's the unmet want?* and let the answers point the way. More important, to keep the customers you have, ask them the platinum questions, *How are we doing?* and *How can we get better?* and let their answers be your guide. And most important, no matter what your job is, work hard every day at making each moment of truth a rewarding one for your customers. Because the bottom line is simply this:

A satisfied customer is the best business strategy of them all.

Summary of How to Win Customers and Keep Them For Life

The Basics

- The secret to winning and keeping customers is to *reward* them.
- Forget about selling. People love to buy but hate to be sold. Concentrate on helping customers buy what's best for them.
- The greatest customer you'll ever win is *you,* because the best salesperson is the true believer.
- The only two things people ever buy are good feelings and solutions to problems.
- Whenever you have contact with a customer, *you are the company* to that customer.
- It's not enough to give the customer excellent service. You must subtly make him aware of the great service he is getting.
- To win new customers, ask the golden question: *"What's the unmet want?"*
- To keep them for life, ask the platinum questions: *"How are we doing?"* and *"How can we get better?"*
- The five best ways to keep customers coming back are: *Be Reliable, be Credible, be Attractive, be Responsive and be Empathic.* "Reliable care" keeps customers coming back.

Managing the Moments of Truth

When the Customer:	*Reward Him:*
1. Appears, calls or inquires	1. By being prompt and prepared
2. Is angry or defensive	2. With kindness and empathy

3. Has special requests	3. By customizing
4. Can't make up his mind	4. With a specific recommendation
5. Raises obstacles or objections to buying	5. By agreeing, empathizing and building value
6. Gives buying signals	6. By reinforcing the signal, making it easy to buy, and asking for the business
7. Buys	7. By delivering more than you promise
8. Refuses to buy	8. With polite appreciation
9. Complains	9. With fast, positive action
10. Is going to be disappointed	10. With positive perks

To manage any moment of truth, ask yourself the winning question: *How can I make him glad he talked to me?* and put the answer to work. Practice the plus, minus, zero theory at every moment of truth.

The Triple-Win Reward System

Implications from the Greatest Management Principle in the World:

- Companies that give excellent service reward employees for providing it.
- If your quality of service is poor, ask the magic question: *What's being rewarded?* Chances are that your employees are being rewarded for something other than taking care of the customer.
- Rewarding the customer is everybody's job. Rewarding those who reward the customer is management's job. How customers get treated is a direct reflection of how management is treating employees.

To keep your team focused on rewarding the customer, find the answer to these four questions and put them to work:

- What behavior and results do I want?
- How will I measure it?
- How will I reward it when I get it?
- How can I show them that the customer comes first?

The quality customer service action plan for managers:

- Treat your customers like lifetime partners.
- Ask everyone where you work for service improvement ideas.
- If you don't have a service strategy, get one.
- Carefully select and heavily train your front-line service people.
- Set service quality goals and rewards.
- Get out of your office and find out what's happening.
- Always be patient but never be satisfied.

The bottom line: A satisfied customer is the best business strategy of all.

Postscript

What's Your Favorite Way to Win and Keep Customers?

In this book, I have given you the best ideas and experiences that I
know of for winning and keeping customers. But I would like for
this book to be just a starting point. I want to give you and others
even more information on how to create new customers and keep
the ones you have.

Do you have a favorite way of rewarding your customers or of
rewarding your employees for rewarding the customer? Have you
found a great way to manage a moment of truth that I didn't mention? What's the single most important ingredient you have found
for increasing the quality of customer service where you work?
Please share your discoveries and success stories with me. Write and
tell me the best, worst, most useful, and funniest experiences you
have ever witnessed involving winning and keeping (or losing) customers. Type up your thoughts and mail them to:

Michael LeBoeuf
P.O. Box 9504
Metairie, LA 70055

Be sure to include your mailing address and preferably a telephone number. Should I plan to use your example in my next book,
I will contact you for permission and to verify the material. Your
reward will be a copy of the new book. If you want confidentiality,
names and places will be changed to insure your anonymity. However, if you want your name included in the acknowledgments, I

shall be happy to do so. Thanks for sharing your experiences with me. And even if you have no experiences to share, I would still like to hear from you about what you did or didn't like about this book. You're my customer and I would like some answers to the platinum questions.

Best regards,
Michael LeBoeuf

INDEX

Accountability, 151
Active reading, 18
Advancement rewards, 162
Age range of customers, 54
Agreement, empathic, 108,
    110–15
Albrecht, Karl, 148, 157
American Express, 133
Amiel, Henri Frederic, 45
"And then some" principle, 123
Angry customers, 91–96
Anthony, Robert, 66
Apologizing for mistakes, 141
Apple Computers, 102, 105,
    119, 128
Arnold, Debra, 86
Atari Computers, 128
Attractiveness, 77
Aubert, Fred, 29–32
Austin, Nancy, 66–67

Ball, Lucille, 130–31
Bargains, 43
Behavior
    consequences of, 25
    mirroring, 49
Beliefs, communication of,
    35–37
Bellus, Dan, 107
Berra, Yogi, 27, 60
Berry, Leonard L., 74, 154
Best Seller!, The (Willingham),
    111
Better than selling principle,
    32–33
Bishop, Bill, 41
Bits and Pieces magazine, 59
Blanchard, Ken, 176
Body language, 49
Bonuses, 158–60, 174
Brainstorming, 33, 62

Bullis, Harry, 32–33
Buying signals, 116–21

Carlzon, Jan, 81, 158
Carnegie, Andrew, 123
Charm, 45
Chester, Ben, 170
Churchill, Winston, 132
Cimberg, Alan, 103
Clark, Frank A., 81
Clemens, Samuel, 116
Closing, 117, 119–21
Coca-Cola Company, 128
Commissions, 158, 159
Competence, customer
    evaluation of, 87
Complaints, 91–96, 133–38
  toll free number for, 55–56
Compliments, 48–49
Conditional rewards, 158
Congress, 149
Consistent performance, 75–76
Consumer Reports, 110
Content analysis, 63
Corporate boards of
    executives, 149
Covey, Steven, 47–48
Credibility, 76–77
Crocker Bank, 57
Customer profiles, 54
Customizing, 97–101

Decision making
  authority for, 103–4
  reinforcement of, 124

stress of, 103, 119
Defensive customers, 91–96
Delta Air Lines, 51, 57
Disney, Walt, 40, 51, 170
Disneyworld, 54

Ebony magazine, 61
Edison, Thomas, 123
Educational level of customers,
    54
Emerson, Ralph Waldo, 23
Emotional bank account,
    47–48
Emotions, 35–36
  buying decisions based on,
    39–44
Empathy, 78
  with complaints, 93–96
  with objections to buying,
    108, 110–15
Estimates, exceeding, 140, 142
Ex-customers, feedback from,
    70, 73
Expectations
  communication of, 155
  exceeding, 122–26
  negative versus positive, 37
  unrealistic, 55, 140
Express Mail, 75–76
Eye contact, 49

Failures, coping with, 128–29
Federal Express, 75, 76, 170
Feedback, 157, 169

Feedback (*cont.*)
  from ex-customers, 70, 73
Feel, felt, found formula,
    111–12
Fields, W. C., 132, 156
First contacts, 83–90
First Union National Bank
    (Charlotte, NC), 141
Five Easy Pieces (film), 97, 100
Flattery, 43
  sincere, 49
Follow-up calls, 95, 125
Ford, Henry, 98, 128
Ford Motor Company, 170
Fortune magazine, 30
Foster, Willa A., 177
Freedom rewards, 162
Front-line employees, 151
  training of, 171–73
Fun as incentive, 163

General Electric, 133
General Mills, 32
General Motors, 62, 98, 133
Gillette, King, 128
Gillette Company, 61
Glad emotional state, 40–42,
    44
Goal setting, 155–56, 173–75
Golden question, 59–64
Good feelings, providing, 39,
    40
Graham, Billy, 87
Graham, Katharine, 34
*Greatest Management Principle
    in the World, The*
    (LeBoeuf), 148
Guarantees, 43, 110, 119, 160

Hallmark Cards, 170
Halverson, Kaye, 47
Hartmarx clothing, 30
Harvard Business School, 38
Helping people to buy, 31–32
Henry, Robert, 84–85
Hess, Karen, 47
Hewlett-Packard, 128
Heyerdahl, Thor, 26
Hill, Napoleon, 123–24
Hilton Hotels, 62
Holiday Inns, 62
Hubbard, Elliott, 96
Humor, 49–50
Hunter, Joseph, 91
Hyatt Hotels, 56–57

IBM, 39, 43, 48, 51, 56, 62, 64,
    123
Importance, feelings of, 43
Income level of customers, 54
Indecision, 102–6
Influence, 50
Informed customers, 57

Japanese companies, 64
Jet magazine, 61
Johnson, John H., 61

Kaufman, George S., 97
Kettering, Charles, 128–29
Kindness, 92–96
King, William, 48
Knowledge, ingrained, 19

L. L. Bean, 85
Lagniappe, 122, 124
L'Amour, Louis, 129
Laughter, 49–50
Leeds, Dorothy, 165
Leonard, Stew, 133
Levitt, Theodore, 38, 63
Life style of customer, 54
Lincoln Continental, 111, 114
Liquid Paper Corporation, 61
Listening skills, 89, 94, 137
Logic, 35, 36
   to justify buying decisions,
      39–40, 43–44
Logs, 19
London, Robert, 102

MacArthur, Gen. Douglas,
      87–88, 128
McDonald, Claude, 63
McDonald's, 62, 75
McGraw–Hill Research, 129
Macintosh, 102, 105, 119
Macy, R. H., 128
Mad emotional state, 40–44
   See also Angry customers
Mail inquiries, 86
Marcus, Stanley, 44
Marital status of customers, 55
Market share, 53
Markets, defining, 61–62
Marriott, J. W., Jr., "Bill,"
      147, 164
Marriott Corporation, 147, 164
Marshall Field and Company,
      162
Masai, J., 139
Megatrends (Naisbitt), 63

Mescon, Michael, 15
Mescon, Timothy, 15
Mirroring behavior, 49
Mitchelson, Theo, 136–37
Mixon, Bud, 159, 175
Mixon Tire Company, 159
Modjeska, Helena, 36
Moments of truth, 17–18,
      81–82
   identification of, 19
Monetary rewards, 159–61
Montgomery Securities, 102
Motives, customers', 168
Mullikin, Harry, 170

Naisbitt, John, 63
Names, using, 49
National Bank of Detroit, 141
National Speakers Association,
      35
Need, absence of, 109
Negative expectations, 37
Neighborhood Walk program,
      164
Neiman-Marcus, 44, 57
Nesmith, Bette, 60–61
New products and services,
      59–64
Nicholson, Jack, 97
Nidetch, Jean, 59, 60
Nonverbal buying signals, 118

Objections and obstacles to
      buying, 107–15
Occupation of customers, 54

Office of Consumer Affairs, 133
On-the-spot rewards, 158
Organization charts, 167–68
Ostrich syndrome, 66

Pacific-Northwest Bell Telephone Company, 29
Paralysis-by-analysis syndrome, 103
Parasuraman, A., 74, 154
Parker, Paul, 119
Passion for Excellence, A (Peters and Austin), 66–67
Pay, performance-based, 159–60
Peale, Norman Vincent, 163
Perception, customer's, 51–58
    improving, 66
Performance measurement, 156–58
Perry, Larry, 61–62
Persistence, 132
Personal growth, 162
Personal space, 49
Personal touch, 50
Personalized service, 56–57
Persuasion, 35, 37
Peters, Tom, 66–67
Piece rates, 159
Platinum questions, 65–73, 125, 135
Polaroid, 133
Positive expectations, 37
Positive perks, 141–42
Posture, 49
Praise, 158, 160–61

Preparation, 85–90
Price objection, 111, 115
Prizes, 163
Problem-solving approach, 44
Problems
    angry response to, 93–96
    handling, 55–56
    identification of, 59–64
    matching solutions with, 89–90
Professionalism, 100–101
Profit-sharing plans, 162
Promotions, 158, 162
Promptness, 85–90

Quality service groups, 172–73
Quanex Corporation, 160
Questions, customers', 86–87

Rapport, establishing, 49, 50, 62, 108, 119
Reagan, Ronald, 36
Recognition, 48–49, 158, 160–61
Recommendations, 102–6
Record keeping, 125
    on complaints, 135–36
Referrals, 125
Refusals, 127–32
Reliability, 75–76
Responsiveness, 77
Return on sales, 53
Rewards
    for customers, 26–28, 59, 64, 81–82, 85, 90, 141–42

for employees, 16, 18, 19,
   147–77
Right touch, 41–44
Risk, 61, 62
Robert, Cavett, 35
Rodgers, Francis (Buck), 39,
   123
Runner's World magazine, 56
Ruth, Kent, 29

Sad emotional state, 40–42, 44
Sanborn, Mark, 83–84, 141–42
Sandburg, Carl, 67
Satisfaction measurements,
   66–73
Scandinavian Airline System
   (SAS), 81–82, 158
Scared emotional state, 40–42,
   44, 119
Scheduled appointments, being
   on time for, 86
Scoggin, Daniel R., 27–28, 65
"Seagull Management," 176
Seed money, 63
Self-image, customer's, 47, 48
Selling, traditional, 31–32
Service, 15, 19, 23, 26
   and attractiveness, 77
   consistent, 75–76
   and credibility, 76–77
   customer recognition of, 17
   customized, 97–101
   decline in, 27
   empathic, 78
   exceeding expectations
      about, 123–26
   measurement of quality of,
      67–73

perception of, 51–58, 66
reputation for, 74
responsive, 77
rewarding employees for,
   151–77
Service America! (Albrecht and
   Zemke), 157
Seuss, Dr., 128
7-Eleven stores, 68, 163, 164
Sex of customers, 54
Sharper Image, The, 51,
   55–56, 110
Shaw, George Bernard, 42,
   130
Sheraton Saint Louis Hotel,
   160–61
Siegel, Fred, 102–3
Sincerity, 49
Singer, Isaac, 42
Six magic words, 112–13
Slogans, 170, 171
Smiling, 49
Smoke screens, 113–14
Solutions, providing, 39, 41,
   43, 44
Southland Corporation, 68,
   163, 164
Special requests, 97–101
Stance, relaxed, 49
State Farm Insurance, 136,
   137, 170
Staying in touch, 57, 62, 125
Strategic Planning Institute, 53
Success Syndrome, 27, 28, 177
Surprise rewards, 158

Tact, 49
Tarson, Ron, 161

Telephone inquiries, 86
Telephone surveys, 68–69
Testimonials, 43, 125
Texas A&M University, 74
TGI Friday's, Inc., 27–28, 65, 100, 141, 144
Thalheimer, Richard, 51, 56
Thanks a Million contest, 163
Think and Grow Rich (Hill), 123
Time off rewards, 162
Toll-free numbers, 55–56, 133
Top management, 135, 149, 151, 174
Touching, nonthreatening, 49
Training, 171–73
Trend-spotting, 63
Trisler, Hank, 120–21
Trust, lack of, 108–9
Twain, Mark, 116

U.S. Post Office, 75–76
Unmet wants, identification of, 59–64, 100

Value
building, 108–15

perceived, 124
Van Buren, Abigail, 93, 127
Verbal buying signals, 117
Visual inventory, 54–55

Walker Research, Inc., 67–68
Watson, Thomas, 48, 64
Weight Watchers International, 59–60, 62
West, Mae, 116
Westin Hotels and Resorts, 170
Wexler, Phil, 99
Whirlpool Corporation, 57
Willingham, Ron, 111–12
Wilson, Debra, 163
Wilson, Woodrow, 123
Winston, Harry, 34–35
Wolfe, Tom, 41
Working Smart (LeBoeuf), 29

Yes-but customers, 113–14

Zeithaml, Valarie A., 74, 154
Zemke, Ron, 148, 157
Ziglar, Zig, 115

About the Author

Companies ranging from "Fortune 500"–sized corporations to small banks and medical practices turn to Dr. Michael LeBoeuf when they want solid, practical ways to live and work smarter. He is an internationally published author, a business consultant, and a dynamic professional speaker and seminar leader. In addition to his writing, consulting, and speaking roles, Dr. LeBoeuf is Professor Emeritus of Management at the University of New Orleans.

His previous books, *Working Smart, Imagineering,* and *Getting Results!,* have been published in numerous foreign-language editions, selected by major book clubs, and excerpted in newspapers and magazines from New York to Bangkok. In addition, both audio and video adaptations of his books have been published, including *How to Win Customers and Keep Them for Life,* which is available as a complete video-based training seminar from Cally Curtis Company of Hollywood.

In constant demand as a speaker, Dr. LeBoeuf addresses business and professional audiences worldwide on the subjects of time management, innovation, rewards-based management, and how to win and keep customers. He has appeared on hundreds of radio and television programs, including *Good Morning America* and the *CBS Evening News.* As both a speaker and a writer, his ability to communicate with clarity and enthusiasm make him a popular favorite.